P9-AET-914

Meditations from the Oratory

PRAYING
WITH THE
CREED

Fr. Benedict J.
Groeschel, C.F.R.

Meditations from the Oratory

PRAYING
WITH THE
CREED

Fr. Benedict J. Groeschel, C.F.R.

Our Sunday Visitor Publishing Division
Our Sunday Visitor, Inc.
Huntington, Indiana 46750

The Scripture citations contained in this work are taken from the *Catholic Edition of the Revised Standard Version of the Bible* (RSV), copyright © 1965 and 1966 by the Division of Christian Education of the National Council of the Churches of Christ in the United States of America. Used by permission. All rights reserved.

Every reasonable effort has been made to determine copyright holders of excerpted materials and to secure permissions as needed. If any copyrighted materials have been inadvertently used in this work without proper credit being given in one form or another, please notify Our Sunday Visitor in writing so that future printings of this work may be corrected accordingly.

Copyright © 2007 by Our Sunday Visitor Publishing Division
Our Sunday Visitor, Inc.   Published 2007

12 11 10 09 08 07   1 2 3 4 5 6 7 8 9

All rights reserved. With the exception of short excerpts for critical reviews, no part of this work may be reproduced or transmitted in any form or by any means whatsoever without permission in writing from the publisher. Write:

Our Sunday Visitor Publishing Division
Our Sunday Visitor, Inc.
200 Noll Plaza
Huntington, IN 46750

ISBN 978-1-59276-321-4 (Inventory No. T420)
LCCN: 2007923457

Cover design by Rebecca J. Heaston
Interior design by Sherri L. Hoffman

Cover photo by Scala / Art Resource, NY
Museo del Prado, Madrid, Spain

PRINTED IN CHINA

Question the beauty of the earth, question the beauty of the sea, question the beauty of the air distending and diffusing itself, question the beauty of the sky ... question all these realities. All respond: "See, we are beautiful." Their beauty is a profession. These beauties are subject to change. Who made them if not the Beautiful One who is not subject to change?

— SAINT AUGUSTINE

Contents

Introduction

This book is the first of four volumes outlining prayer meetings for devout Catholics. It contains weekly meditations first composed for prayer groups who wished to meditate and pray together on the truths of the Catholic faith. The first of such groups in history, made up of devout informed laity, goes back to the late fifteenth century, which was a time of great turmoil and scandal in the Church. A number of priests and people, under the inspiration of Saint Catherine of Genoa (1447–1510), banded together to study the Bible and Church teachings, joining their study to a life of serious prayer and good works. A laywoman known as Caterinetta Fieschi Adorna, Saint Catherine was director of the Pammatone, in Genoa, the largest charity hospital in the world. She and her spiritual followers called the first prayer groups Oratories of Divine Love. The Italian word for prayer group is *oratorio*, which in turn is derived from the Latin word for prayer, *oratio*.

The Oratory of Divine Love was revived in America at the beginning of the new millennium as part of an effort by the Franciscan Friars of the Renewal to encourage Church reform.

Although these meditations, which comprise the first of four volumes, were written specifically for the Oratory, the simple outline and structure are not restricted to the Oratory or its members. We hope that they will be helpful to all who wish to grow in their faith and in the love of God and neighbor. Any group of devout people can grow and learn using these meditations, whether at weekly meetings or even on their own.

Members of the Oratory today, as in the past, bind themselves to lead a devout life, to reverent participation in the liturgy, and to virtuous works of charity and religion. Oratorians still take on these good works, for example, helping out at soup kitchens and other works for the needy, visiting the sick and homebound, and regular friendly visits to the elderly. Today works of religion can include pro-life activities, assisting in a parish, especially in religious education, or being Eucharistic minister to the homebound.

These books of Oratory meditations will be published, one volume annually, for the next four years to make a complete cycle of Catholic faith and Scripture. They will correspond to the four parts of the *Catechism of the Catholic Church*:

    Book I. The Profession of Faith
    Book II. The Celebration of the Christian Mystery

Book III. Life in Christ
Book IV. Christian Prayer

It would be helpful for readers of these books to have at hand a copy of the *Catechism*, with which they will become familiar.

Although not coextensive with or structured according to the liturgical year, the meditations in this first book coincide at times with major liturgical feasts and seasons. They begin with the first Sunday of Lent and go on through Easter and Pentecost. Oratorians or others using this book in groups can begin or pick up at any point. Those who meet only sporadically should try to cover each of the meditations given here, even if on their own. It is advisable to limit meetings to an hour, or perhaps an hour and a half, to avoid tedium. It is important to keep in mind that the overall plan for this series is to follow the *Catechism* with its four major divisions.

The original Oratories selected a reader who served for six months and coordinated the meeting. A group may also suggest someone as a permanent secretary, who corresponds with a central Oratory and tends to simple business matters, such as where meetings will be held, and circulates information about sick or needy members. It is intended that the structure and operations of the Oratory be very simple.

The meditations in this volume are composed by me. In later volumes I am blessed to have the assistance of Yolanda and Jerry Cleffi, who care for the office of the Oratory and maintain the Oratory's web site. The Cleffis are converts to the Church, having served for some years as ministers of the Assembly of God. Both hold master's degrees in theology from Saint Joseph's Seminary (New York). I feel that Divine Providence brought us together and that they provided a great service to the Oratory when I suffered a near-fatal auto accident and required many months of recovery.

Whether you belong to the Oratory or not, we hope that you will find this book spiritually beneficial. Further, we hope that the serious study of the Scriptures and the Catholic faith will make you a deeper witness to the saving grace of Our Lord Jesus Christ and an active participant in the work of reform of the Church. Reform is just beginning and can be seen particularly in the young people known as the John Paul II generation. There is much to do, as Pope Benedict XVI has indicated: the restoration of a sense of awe and reverence; the renewal of Catholic education, which is often mediocre when not positively destructive; the strengthening of the priesthood with the resurrection of religious life; and the work of loving care for the poor and unfortunate.

Don't think of the prayer groups as a small beginning. Professor John Olin, a distinguished historian, has written:

> Sometime between 1514 and 1517 a branch of this Oratory was established in Rome — an event which Pastor and other historians have singled out as marking the beginning of effective Catholic reform in this troubled age.[1]

There is a serious movement in the diocese of Genoa at the present time to propose Saint Catherine as a doctor of the Church. This initiative has been strengthened by the interest of former archbishops of Genoa: Cardinal Tarcisio Bertone, S.D.B., who is now papal secretary of state, and the late Cardinal Giuseppe Siri. Were Catherine so honored, she would be the first married laywoman to receive that title. We Oratorians hope that she will be so recognized because her spiritual teachings, particularly her doctrine on purgatory, have deeply affected the Catholic Church for several centuries. We hope that you will read about Saint Catherine and get to know this remarkable person, who can be said to have begun the Catholic Reformation. Her mystical teachings on purgatory presenting this belief positively as a motive for gratitude, hope, and love are most refreshing and encouraging. Her profound influence on the Protestant Holiness movement in the nineteenth century is a remarkable chapter in ecumenical relations. Any serious Christian will be deeply moved by her spiritual writings and her life.[2]

In the meantime your, participation in the weekly Oratory meditations may prove spiritually beneficial to you or to your group. If they do, we would be grateful to hear from you at the Oratory:

Oratory of Divine Love
P.O. Box 1465
Bloomfield, NJ 07003

The Nicene Creed

I believe in one God, the Father, the Almighty,
maker of heaven and earth,
of all that is seen and unseen.
I believe in one Lord, Jesus Christ,
the only Son of God, eternally begotten of the
 Father,
God from God, Light from Light, true God from
 true God,
begotten, not made, one in Being with the Father.
Through Him all things were made.
For us men and for our salvation, He came down
 from heaven:
by the power of the Holy Spirit He was born of the
 Virgin Mary, and became man.
For our sake He was crucified under Pontius Pilate;
 He suffered, died, and was buried.
On the third day He rose again in fulfillment of the
 Scriptures;

He ascended into heaven and is seated at the right
    hand of the Father.
He will come again in glory to judge the living and
    the dead,
and His kingdom will have no end.
I believe in the Holy Spirit, the Lord, the giver of life,
who proceeds from the Father and the Son.
With the Father and the Son He is worshipped and
    glorified.
He has spoken through the Prophets.
I believe in one holy catholic and apostolic Church.
I acknowledge one baptism for the forgiveness of sins.
I look for the resurrection of the dead,
and the life of the world to come.
Amen.

Meditation One

I Believe in God (#1)

READINGS

John 14 (whole chapter); Romans 11:33 and 12:1–21

We begin our weekly meditation with the very first words of the Apostles' Creed. What does it mean to believe in God? Since faith is a gift, it means two things: accepting this gift and deciding to believe.

Saint Thomas Aquinas tells us that the existence of God is not a self-evident fact, like the passage of time or the laws of the physical universe — for instance, gravity. We must use our reason in order to conclude that this wonderful world or the cosmos we live in, from the tiniest cells to the incredible galaxies of hundreds of billions of stars, has a Creator. His power and intelligence is completely beyond the grasp of our minds; even the greatest of all human intelligence would be far below what is necessary to grasp God's being. Articles on the origin of the universe should bring any thoughtful person to a complete and awesome silence.

But this is only the beginning of faith. We do not believe in some world force or creative power unconcerned with us; rather we believe in a heavenly Father.

The acceptance of a "personal God" depends on the gift of faith. If you wish to believe, you must accept the gift of faith joyfully and embrace it by saying, "I believe in God the Father Almighty."

In these unbelieving times it is necessary to say this over and over again, and to say with the apostles, "Lord, increase our faith."

Quotation for Meditation

I come then to this conclusion: If I must submit my mind to mysteries, it is not much matter whether it is a mystery more or a mystery less, when faith anyhow is the very essence of all religion, when the main difficulty to an inquirer is firmly to hold that there is a Living God, in spite of the darkness which surrounds him, the Creator and Witness and Judge of all. When once the mind is broken in, as it must be to the belief in a power above itself; when once it understands that it is not itself the measure of all things in heaven and on earth the mind will have little difficulty going forward. I do not say it can go on to other truths without convictions. I do not say it ought to believe the Catholic faith without grounds and motives, but I say that when once the mind believes in God the great obstacle to faith has been taken away — a proud and self-sufficient spirit. When once a person with the eyes of his soul and by the power of divine grace recognizes his Creator he has passed a line, and that has happened to him that cannot happen twice. He has bent his stiff neck, he has triumphed over himself.

— John Henry Newman, *Discourses to Mixed Congregations* (See also *The Journey Toward God*, 67–68)

Quiet Time and Then Discussion

Questions for Meditation

1. When I think of God, how do I think of Him?
2. How do I respond to all the unbelief around me?
3. Am I willing to be a witness to faith, so that when God gives the grace, I am there for the person who is moving toward belief?
4. Do I try to increase my own faith by reverent prayer?

Prayer

Heavenly Father, I believe in You, although Your being is surrounded by mystery. It is difficult for us to grasp the limitations of what we can know, much less enter into direct knowledge of Your being. Give me the grace of the Holy Spirit to be in reverent awe in Your presence. Your Son has told us that You are our Father. I choose by Your grace to believe in You. Not to believe in You is to fall into impenetrable darkness; but to believe in You is to walk in the brightness of light that makes suffering endurable, life worthwhile, and eternal life with You my hope beyond all others. Amen.

Meditation Two

I Believe in God (#2)

READINGS:
John 3:1–21 (read slowly); Ephesians 1:2–22

When we say we believe in God, we plunge ourselves into the most profound mystery. A mystery is something we know exists, but we are not able to comprehend what it means completely. God is the greatest of all mysteries because of His nature, His existence from all eternity, His infinite power, and His ability to be aware of all things great and small. Of all the people in the ancient world, the Jews had the most profound knowledge of God because He revealed Himself to Abraham and to others in the Old Testament. Jesus, however, revealed things about God that the Jewish scriptures could not reveal. Jesus revealed God as our loving Father, the one who welcomes back the Prodigal Son, the one who sends His beloved Son into the world to save our souls. When we believe, we cast ourselves into the mystery of God, but at the same time into the mystery of God's love. To accept the mystery of God is to pass beyond the commonplace, the limited, the narrow-minded. But we must live up to our belief by not putting anything in the world before God. Then we can love others and enjoy in moderation all the good things He has given us because we have put our faith in God first. Putting things in proper order is what gives people peace.

Quotations for Meditation

The most beautiful and most profound emotion we can experience is the sensation of the mystical. It is the sower of all true science. He to whom this emotion is a stranger, who can no longer wonder and stand rapt in awe, is as good as dead. To know that what is impenetrable to us really exists, manifesting itself as the highest wisdom and the most radiant beauty which our dull faculties can comprehend only in their most primitive forms — this knowledge, this feeling is at the center of true religiousness.

— Albert Einstein, quoted in Lincoln Barnett,
The Universe and Dr. Einstein, 105–106

Far from repudiating Christianity or regarding it with suspicious eyes because of its mysteries, we ought to recognize its divine grandeur in these very mysteries. So essential to Christianity are its mysteries that in its character of truth revealed by the Son of God and the Holy Spirit it would stand convicted of intrinsic contradiction if it brought forward no mysteries. Its Author would carry with Him a poor recommendation for His divinity if He taught us only such truths as in the last analysis we could have learned from a mere man, or could have perceived and adequately grasped by our own unaided powers.

I would go even further: the truths of Christianity would not stir us as they do, nor would they draw us or hearten us, and they would not be embraced by us with such love and joy, if they contained no mysteries.... A truth that is easily discovered and quickly grasped can neither enchant nor hold. To enchant and hold us, it must surprise us by its novelty, it must overpower us with its magnificence; its wealth and profundity must exhibit ever new splendors, ever deeper abysses to the exploring eye.

— Matthias Joseph Scheeben,
The Mysteries of Christianity, 4–5

Quiet Time and Then Discussion

Questions for Meditation

1. Do I think with joy and awe of the mystery of God's love for the world, for you and me, as it is taught by Christ?

2. Do I get confused, disheartened, or even doubtful if people offer arguments against the faith, or if those who represent the faith fail?

3. Do I think of God as the beloved Father of Jesus and learn of God from the face of Jesus in prayer?

Prayer

Heavenly Father, make me aware of Your mysteries and teach me to enjoy their freedom and to reject all doubts on the strength of Your mysteries. You are my Father. You are everything and I am nothing. I rejoice that, as my Father, You have filled my emptiness. Christ is my brother, Savior, and Lord. Give me the grace to acknowledge and to recognize these truths held in mystery. Amen.

Meditation Three

I Believe in God (#3)

READINGS:
Matthew 6:25–34 (read slowly); John 12:20–36

Christians believe not only that God knows each of us individually but that He provides for us in such a way that all that happens to us will contribute to our salvation. This is called the Providence of God. Even when natural catastrophes occur or harmful and destructive things are done by the wickedness of human beings, God will bring out of these events the salvation of souls of those who turn to Him with faith and trust.

In the first reading Our Lord teaches us to trust and not to worry, but in the second reading we see Jesus confronted with His own impending passion and death. He clearly states to the puzzled crowd, "I, when I am lifted up from the earth, will draw all men to myself." The evangelist tells us that He is speaking of His own crucifixion. We will all face natural disasters, even our own death, and most of us will be hurt by others, even those we love. At such times we must believe in God's Providence and trust that for those who love Him, all things will work together for the good.

Quotation for Meditation
The Silent Guide

When God becomes our guide, He insists that we trust Him without reservations and put aside all nervousness about His guidance. We are sent along the path He has chosen for us, but we cannot see it, and nothing we have read is any help to us. Were we acting on our own, we should have to rely on our experience. It would be too risky to do anything else. But it is very different when God acts with us. Divine action is always new and fresh, it never retraces its steps, but always finds new routes. When we are led by this action, we have no idea where we are going, for the paths we tread cannot be discovered from books or by any of our thoughts. But these paths are always opened in front of us and we are impelled along them. Imagine we are in a strange district at night and are crossing fields unmarked by any path, but we have a guide. He asks no advice nor tells us of his plans. So what can we do except trust him? It is no use trying to see where we are, look at maps or question passers-by. That would not be tolerated by a guide who wants us to rely on him. He will get satisfaction from overcoming our fears and doubts, and will insist that we have complete trust in him.

God's activity can never be anything but good, and does not need to be reformed or controlled. It began at the creation of the world and up to now has continued with the same energy which knows no limits. Its fertility is inexhaustible. It does one thing today, another tomorrow, yet it is the same activity which every moment produces constantly fresh results, and it will continue throughout eternity…. If we wish to live according to the Gospel, we must abandon ourselves simply and completely to the action of God. Jesus Christ is its source. He "is the same today as He was yesterday and as He will be forever" (Hebrews 13:8). What He has done is finished, what remains to be done is being carried on every moment. Every saint shares in this divine life, and Jesus Christ, though always the same, is different in each one. The life of each saint is the life of Jesus Christ. It is a new gospel.

— Jean-Pierre de Caussade, S.J.,
Abandonment to Divine Providence, 83–84

◦ Quiet Time and Then Discussion ◦

Questions for Meditation

1. Is God really running the world?
2. Have we ever felt that His Providence has failed us?
3. Do we learn something from the words of Jesus before the Passion in John 12?

Prayer

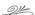

Heavenly Father, I do believe in You and in Your loving Providence. But so much happens that seems to go against this conviction. Give me the grace to persevere in difficulties, even in disasters, so that I may come to see in my own experience how You bring good out of evil. You did this when Your beloved Son faced the Cross and His death and brought salvation to the world out of the worst of evils. Amen.

Meditation Four

I Believe in One God ... Maker ...
of All That Is Seen and Unseen (#4)

READINGS:
John 12:37–50; Romans 4:18–22

These words from the Creed of Nicea, which we say at Mass on Sunday, can have a special meaning for Christians in our unbelieving times. Even with friends and family, we are surrounded by those of little faith and those of no faith. This unbelief is fed by materialism — the prejudice that only physical things exist — and by skepticism — the idea that no one should believe anything that cannot be proven. People use these very narrow ideas and assumptions to deny the existence of the mysterious, absolute, unchanging, infinite, and totally personal God, who allows us to call Him Our Father. We cannot know about the heavenly Father unless He reveals Himself, and the only means we have to accept this revelation is faith. We know from experience that faith can be lost and found again. It can be beautiful and certain, or it can be dark and attacked by doubt. The Christian must walk while there is light. This means we must practice our faith fervently and well in times of blessing. When the darkness of sorrow comes, we will be able to hold out and not be blown off course. Belonging to the Church and to a faith community of friends like the Oratory can be a great help at this time.

Quotation for Meditation

Christianity entered the world as a religion replete with mysteries. It was proclaimed as the mystery of Christ (Rom. 16: 25–27; Col. 1:25–27), as the "mystery of the kingdom of God" (Mark 4:11; Luke 8:10). Its ideas and doctrines were unknown, unprecedented, and they were to remain inscrutable and unfathomable….

Even friends and zealous defenders of Christianity could not always suppress a certain dread when they stood in the obscurity of its mysteries. To buttress belief in Christian truth and to defend it, they desired to resolve it into a rational science, to demonstrate articles of faith by arguments drawn from reason, and so to reshape them that nothing would remain of the obscure, the incomprehensible, the impenetrable. They did not realize that by such a procedure they were betraying Christianity into the hands of her enemies and wresting the fairest jewel from her crown.

The greater, the more sublime, and the more divine Christianity is, the more inexhaustible, inscrutable, unfathomable, and mysterious its subject matter must be. If its teaching is worthy of the only-begotten Son of God, if the Son of God had to descend from the bosom of His Father to initiate us into this teaching, could we expect anything else than the revelation of the deepest mysteries locked up in God's heart? Could we expect anything else than disclosures concerning a higher, invisible world, about divine and heavenly things, which "eye hath not seen, nor ear heard," and which could not enter into the heart of any man (1 Cor. 2:9)? And if God has sent us His own Spirit to teach us all truth, the Spirit of His truth, who dwells in God and there searches the deep things of God (cf. John 16:13; 1 Cor. 2:10f), should this Spirit reveal nothing new, great, and wondrous, should He teach us no sublime secrets?

— Matthias Joseph Scheeben,
The Mysteries of Christianity, 3–4

✎ Quiet Time and Then Discussion ✎

Questions for Meditation

1. Have I mistakenly thought that I had to understand all the teachings of faith?
2. Have I thought about what the mystery of God really is?
3. What is the best response to the mysteries of God?

Prayer

Holy Spirit, give me the grace of continually renewed and growing faith. Let my heart and mind rise into the brightness of divine truth, where I cannot see clearly because of the overwhelming light. Help me, by reverent and prayerful faith, to bear witness to those of little or no faith, so that they may enter into the light of truth. Amen.

I Believe in Jesus Christ, His Only Son (#1)

READINGS:
John 1:1–18; Romans 1:1–7

Every year, Holy Week gives us the opportunity to review the revelation of Jesus of Nazareth about Himself, His relationship to the Father and to the Holy Spirit, His work as Savior and Redeemer, His role as the one true Teacher, as Judge of the living and the dead, as King of Kings and Lord of Lords. It is a tragedy — perhaps the key to all other tragedies that have befallen the Christian world in the last century — that a vibrant devotion to Christ and a profound recognition of Him as the Son of God have eroded. In some places, like Northern Europe, they have almost disappeared. We must begin our meditation on Christ with this realization; otherwise, we will be caught in one of two contemporary pitfalls: Christ will be just an abstract idea of goodness, or even niceness, or He will be the object of devotion that descends into mere sentimentality.

The two Scripture readings powerfully call us to begin by acknowledging that Jesus Christ, Child of Mary, is a divine Person. He is the Son of the Father and Creator of All, the Living God. Only fervent prayer can open this incredible mystery to us.

Quotation for Meditation

At first a child like any other, it cries, is hungry, sleeps, and yet is "the Word . . . become flesh." It cannot be said that God "inhabits" this infant, however gloriously; or that heaven has set its seal upon him, so that he must pursue it, suffer for it in a manner sublimely excelling all other contacts between God and man; this child *is* God in essence and in being.

If an inner protest should arise here, give it room. It is not good to suppress anything; if we try to, it only goes underground, becomes toxic, and reappears later in far more obnoxious form. Does anyone object to the whole idea of God-become-man? Is he willing to accept the Incarnation only as a profound and beautiful allegory, never as literal truth? If doubt can establish a foothold anywhere in our faith, it is here. Then we must be patient and reverent, approaching this central mystery of Christianity with calm, expectant, prayerful attention; one day its sense will be revealed to us. In the meantime, let us remember the directive "But love does such things!"

— Romano Guardini, *The Lord*, 16

✒ Quiet Time and Then Discussion ✒

Questions for Meditation

1. Do I stop sometimes to think of the mystery and the incredible fact that a Divine Person became a human child?
2. Do I really show my gratitude to Jesus for His coming into this difficult world?
3. Do I try to tell others about Him?

Prayer

Lord Jesus Christ, I do not take seriously enough the fact that You came to save us, to save me. Out of all eternity You are God the Word, and You came to save us from everlasting death. Give me the grace of the Holy Spirit that I may try more and more to serve You and follow You, my Lord and my God. Amen.

I Believe in Jesus Christ,
His Only Son (#2)

READINGS:
Luke 1:26–38; Galatians 4:4–7

The mystery of Christ begins with who He is. There have been many conflicts about His Person and what it means for God to become a man. Because of the decline of faith and lack of knowledge about the faith at the present time, there is a real danger that Christians will lose their belief in Christ. By the early fourth century the Gospels and other New Testament writings had been accepted. The Council of Nicea (325) declared that Jesus Christ was "God from God, light from light, True God from True God, begotten not made, one in being with the Father." We proclaim this faith every Sunday at Mass. In 431, in response to the errors of Nestor, the deposed archbishop of Constantinople, the Church made a very important statement: Mary was the mother of a person who was always a divine Person. Christ in his divinity and humanity is one, and that oneness was not a blending of the human and divine, or a compound like water, or a mixture. His human nature (from Mary) and His divine nature as Son of God were joined in a union, which took place by means of His Person (*hypostasis* in Greek), so that this mystery is called the hypostatic union. This dogmatic teaching, along with the proclamation that Mary was the mother of a divine Person, or Mother of God, came from two very important councils, Ephesus (431) and Chalcedon (451). The following decree of Chalcedon is worth serious meditation.

Quotation for Meditation

Following the holy Fathers, we unanimously teach and confess one and the same Son, our Lord Jesus Christ: the same perfect in divinity and perfect in humanity, the same truly God and truly man, composed of rational soul and body; consubstantial with the Father as to his divinity and consubstantial with us as to his humanity; "like us in all things but sin." He was begotten from the Father before all ages as to his divinity and in these last days, for us and for our salvation, was born as to his humanity of the virgin Mary, the Mother of God.[3]

We confess that one and the same Christ, Lord, and only-begotten Son, is to be acknowledged in two natures without confusion, change, division, or separation. The distinction between the natures was never abolished by their union, but rather the character proper to each of the two natures was preserved as they came together in one person (*prosopon*) and one hypostasis.[4]

— As cited in the *Catechism of the Catholic Church*, n. 467

❧ Quiet Time and Then Discussion ❧

Questions for Meditation

1. Is Jesus Christ truly human?
2. Is Jesus Christ truly divine?
3. Is He really a divine Person?
4. What does this mystery say to us about our own humanity?

Prayer

Lord Jesus Christ, Son of God, Son of Mary, I come to the mystery of Your Incarnation with great reverence and awe. Let me never lose this sense of mystery; rather, with the help of the Holy Spirit, help me to grow in the belief that You are truly the Savior of the World, because You are Son of God and Son of Man. Amen.

Meditation Seven

He Suffered Under Pontius Pilate, Was Crucified, Died, and Was Buried

READINGS:

Any account of the Passion (Luke 22:39–23:56 recommended)

The Passion of Christ, which means all the events from the time of the Agony in the Garden to His death on the Cross, has been the fruitful focus of Christian meditation for almost two thousand years. There are so many aspects to it that one should never grow tired of mining the gold in this mystery of the Kingdom. Perhaps the most fruitful meditation would be to ask, What does the suffering of Christ mean to me? It means that the Son of God loved all humanity and each person to such an extent that He was willing to endure all of His suffering for us.

The mystics of the Church have insisted, almost with one voice, that the greatest of Christ's suffering was His taking on in some mysterious way all the evil of the world. He took on all the sin that had been committed, was being committed then, and would continue until the end of the world. "He drank the cup to its bitter dregs." Many reasons are given for His doing this: He chose to be vulnerable in this world to evil, as we all are. He came to our world vulnerable to fulfill God's will for our redemption. He paid the price; He settled the account of justice, which is part of the law of being, often called divine Justice. He gave the example of a perfect love of God and neighbor. He laid down His own life. He gave hope to and shared in the bitter sufferings of all human beings. He became the God who suffers. Why? Because love does such things.

Quotation for Meditation

Ten thousand things come before us one after another in the course of life, and what are we to think of them? What colour are we to give them? Are we to look at all things in a gay and mirthful way? Or in a melancholy way? In a desponding or a hopeful way? Are we to make light of life altogether, or to treat the whole subject seriously? Are we to make greatest things of little consequence, or least things of great consequence? Are we to keep in mind what is past and gone, or are we to look on to the future, or are we to be absorbed in what is present? *How* are we to look at things? This is the question which all persons of observation ask themselves, and answer each in his own way. They wish to think by rule; by something within them, which may harmonize and adjust what is without them. Such is the need felt by reflective minds. Now, let me ask, what *is* the real key, what is the Christian interpretation of this world? What is given us by revelation to estimate and measure this world by? . . . The Crucifixion of the Son of God.

It is the death of the Eternal Word of God made flesh, which is our great lesson how to think and how to speak of this world. His Cross has put its due value upon every thing which we see, upon all fortunes, all advantages, all ranks, all dignities, all pleasures; upon the lust of the flesh, and the lust of the eyes, and the pride of life. It has set a price upon the excitements, the rivalries, the hopes, the fears, the desires, the efforts, the triumphs of mortal man.... It has brought together and made consistent all that seemed discordant and aimless. It has taught us how to live, how to use this world, what to expect, what to desire, what to hope. It is the tone into which all the strains of this world's music are ultimately to be resolved.

— John Henry Newman,
Parochial and Plain Sermons, VI, 7

❧ Quiet Time and Then Discussion ❧

Questions for Meditation

1. What are some of the reasons for Christ's death on the Cross?
2. What practical lessons does the Cross teach me on how to live my life?
3. What does the Cross tell me about God?

Prayer

Lord Jesus Christ, You died for us all and You died for me. That central fact of my life must become more and more paramount in my thinking. I can never exhaust the depths of the mystery of the Redemption. Help me, O Lord, by Your Holy Spirit, and by the words of the Gospel, to appreciate what You did for us on that first Good Friday long ago. Amen.

Meditation Eight

The Third Day He Rose Again
from the Dead

READINGS:
John 20 (whole chapter)

The Resurrection of Jesus and His Ascension into heaven are, along with the Incarnation, the most mysterious events ever to take place on the face of the earth. The Son of God came to this world at the Annunciation as a divine Person coming out of all eternity. He took upon Himself a true human body and a true human soul in the womb of the Blessed Virgin. He united His divine Nature and Person with a human body and soul, so it is proper to say that Jesus of Nazareth is truly the Son of God and equal to the Father in all things. He experienced human death — the separation of His body and soul. His body was placed in the tomb, and His human soul accompanied His divine Person into the lower world, where the just waited for their redemption. On the third day the body and soul and the divine Person were resurrected together, and a totally singular event occurred. A human body, made of the dust of the earth; a human mind, dependent on the body with its central nervous system; and His human soul, all entered everlasting life — the life of God. For the first time a thing of earth became a thing of heaven, of everlasting life. This is really the beginning of our own promise of eternal life. We will rise and live forever only if we are united with Christ, the Eternal Son of God. Without this promise, human life is a bad dream, an unmitigated tragedy. This is why we rejoice. Christ is risen!

Quotation for Meditation

In the Resurrection, that which had lain dormant from the beginning in the vital existence of the Son of Man and God becomes apparent. When we look back on our own existence, it seems like a movement begun in the darkness of childhood — as far back as memory reaches — which mounts gradually to the summit, only, more or less fulfilled or broken off, to descend. The curve of my existence begins with birth and ends with death. Before it lies darkness so complete that it seems incredible that I ever could have begun to exist at all. After it again dark, out of which gropes a vague sensation of hope. In Jesus this is not so. The arch of his existence does not begin with his birth, but reaches far behind it into eternity: "Before Abraham came to be, I am" (John 8:58). These are not the words of a Christian mystic of the second century, as has been claimed, but the direct expression of what was alive in Christ. And the arch does not break off in death, but continues, bearing his earthly existence with it, into eternity: "... and they will kill him; and on the third day he will rise again" (Matthew 17:22). For Christ, death — however burdened and agonizing and essential — is only a passageway to fulfillment. "Did not the Christ have to suffer these things before entering into his glory?" he asks the disciples on the way to Emmaus (Luke 24:26). The Resurrection is the blossoming of the seed he has always borne within him. He who rejects it, rejects everything in Jesus' life and consciousness that is linked with it. What then remains, is not worth faith.

— Romano Guardini, *The Lord*, 477

❧ Quiet Time and Then Discussion ❧

Questions for Meditation

1. Can we think about Christ without thinking about His Resurrection?

2. Is there any other event in human history like the Resurrection?
3. Did Christ have to rise from the dead?

Prayer

Lord Jesus, often in the distractions of life I do not think of Your Resurrection. More frequently I think of Your sufferings because You unite Yourself with us. The Resurrection is mysterious and must remain beyond us until we enter eternal life, and yet it is our sole and singular and supreme hope. Without the Resurrection there is no hope, no hope of eternal life, no hope of surviving death, no hope that we will see our dear ones in the next world. All our hope, O Christ, is in You alone. Give us Your grace, that we may grow in hope and never be disappointed in that hope. We pray through Christ our Lord. Amen.

Meditation Nine

Christ From Above

READINGS:
Luke 24:13–43; John 21:9–14

For a number of decades there has been a growing tendency to study the life of Christ, as it is presented to us in the Gospels, from a starting point that is, I think, dangerous to faith. This procedure is referred to as Christology from below. It means beginning with the idea that Jesus of Nazareth was an interesting historical figure and asking the question, Why does anyone even know His name after two thousand years? Such a procedure results in an erosion of the whole Christian doctrine about Jesus Christ and leads to widespread loss of faith in the Christian world. The other starting point is called Christianity from above. It begins with the magnificent structure of understandings and interpretations based on the Scriptures and carefully integrated from one teaching to the next. This approach is proposed in both

Catholic and Orthodox Churches and is cherished by many
Protestants, especially Evangelicals.

In the readings we have selected for our meditation, it is
obvious that the mystery of Christ continued even after His
death and is shown not only in His Resurrection but also in His
appearances before His Ascension into heaven. This was a completely different kind of human presence. Christ appeared to
His disciples when they were behind locked doors. The disciples
at Emmaus did not immediately recognize Him when He walked
with them on the road. Christ appeared and disappeared at will,
with no effort at journeying to any particular place. But the
early Church strongly asserted and believed that the real Jesus of
Nazareth was seen after His Resurrection, not an apparition of
His body or a ghost. The first proof that He was not a ghost is
that He ate a piece of fish and even prepared a meal for others.
The devout Christian will see Christ from above, as the Word
made flesh who came to dwell among us.

Quotation for Meditation

Contemplating the mystery of the Incarnation of the Son of
God, the Church prepares to cross the threshold of the third millennium. Never more than at this time do we feel the need to
make our own the Apostle's hymn of praise and thanksgiving:

"Blessed be the God and Father of our Lord Jesus Christ, who has blessed us in Christ with every spiritual blessing in the heavenly places, even as he chose us in him before the foundation of the world that we should be holy and blameless before him. He destined us in love to be his sons through Jesus Christ, according to the purpose of his will…. For he has made known to us in all wisdom and insight the mystery of his will, according to his purpose which he set forth in Christ as a plan for the fullness of time, to unite all things in him, things in heaven and things on earth" (Eph. 1:3–5, 9–10).

These words clearly indicate that in Jesus Christ the history of salvation finds its culmination and ultimate meaning. In him, we have all received "grace upon grace" (John 1:16), having been reconciled with the Father (cf. Rom. 5:10; 2 Cor 5:18). The birth of Jesus at Bethlehem is not an event which can be consigned to the past. The whole of human history, in fact, stands in reference to Him; our own time and the future of the world are illumined by His presence. He is "the Living One" (Rev. 1:18), "who is, who was and who is to come" (Rev. 1:4). Before Him every knee must bend, in the heavens, on earth and under the earth, and every tongue proclaim that He is Lord (cf. Phil. 2:10–11). In the encounter with Christ, every man discovers the mystery of his own life.

Jesus is the genuine newness which surpasses all human expectations, and such He remains for ever, from age to age. The Incarnation of the Son of God and the salvation which He has accomplished by His death and Resurrection are therefore the true criterion for evaluating all that happens in time and every effort to make life more human.

— Pope John Paul II, *Incarnationis Mysterium*
(The Mystery of the Incarnation), 1

ᦂ Quiet Time and Then Discussion ᦂ

Questions for Meditation

1. Is Jesus Christ just an ordinary person, chosen by God, and possessing great virtue?
2. Is Jesus Christ the eternal Son of God made man?
3. How could you explain this to someone who thinks that Jesus is simply a very good person or even the best person who ever lived?

Prayer

Holy Spirit, without You we cannot say, "Jesus Christ is Lord." Yet the salvation of the world depends on Him; in fact, all human history unfolds for and with Him. Holy Spirit, without Your sevenfold gifts we cannot know, appreciate, believe in, or proclaim this fact of salvation. Fill us with faith in Jesus Christ as Lord. Amen.

Meditation Ten

Christ in His Miracles

READINGS:
John 6:1–12; John 9:1–41

Beginning with the marriage feast at Cana, when Jesus transformed about 160 gallons of water into fine wine (this first of signs, as Saint John calls it), the life of Christ is filled with accounts of miracles. In the last century or so, the actual signs of divine power, consistently described as facts in the Gospels, have been gratuitously and flatly denied by unbelievers; they have been more carefully and subtly denied by some believing scholars. Removing the accounts of Christ's miracles from the Gospels with a razor blade leaves us with a pile of confetti and a most unconvincing narrative. Why should anyone believe in Him?

Congregations continue to be disedified and their faith undermined by these denials. Those who deny the historical reality of Christ's miracles have been summed up in a single phrase by Pope John Paul II in his teachings published as *Wonders and Signs*. He states that people reject the historicity of the Gospel accounts because of a prejudice against the supernatural. The devout Christian will have no trouble believing in the supernatural acts of Christ (called miracles, which means marvelous events). They accept without hesitation that the Scriptures are given to us under the inspiration of the Holy Spirit and are essentially without error and meant to be our guides on the road to salvation. Miracles occur even in our own times. I know people who made marvelous recoveries, and I have known people like the venerable Father Solanus Casey, O.F.M. Cap., who performed miraculous healings through the power of God (see Mark 16:14–18). Scientific procedures can neither affirm nor deny the miraculous, because science studies the predictable and the measurable. Science can only certify that a healing took place but cannot give a scientific explanation. Faced with substantial disputes about the miracles of Christ, believers should simply cite the brief statement of the Holy Father given here and pray for an increase of faith for those who have little faith. Christ often rebuked His own disciples for having little faith, and we are all in danger of this one way or another. We need to make our own the prayer of the disciples: "Lord, increase our faith."

Quotation for Meditation

On the day of Pentecost, after receiving the light and power of the Holy Spirit, Peter bore clear and courageous witness to Christ crucified and risen. "Men of Israel," he proclaimed, "hear these words: Jesus of Nazareth, a man attested to you by God with mighty works and wonders and signs … you crucified … and killed. But God raised him up, releasing him from the pangs of death" (cf. Acts 2:22–24).

This testimony includes a synthesis of the whole messianic activity of Jesus of Nazareth, whom God had commended by "mighty deeds, wonders and signs." It also constitutes an outline of the first Christian catechesis, offered to us by the very head of the apostolic college, Peter.…

Before proceeding step by step in analyzing the significance of these "wonders and signs" (as Peter had very specifically defined them on the day of Pentecost), one must note that they (the wonders and signs) certainly pertain to the integral content of the Gospels as eyewitness testimonies to Christ. It is not in fact possible to exclude the mighty deeds from the gospel text and context. The analysis of not only the text but also of the context speaks in favor of their "historical" character; it attests that they are facts which actually happened, and that they were really performed by Christ. Whoever approaches the matter with intellectual honesty and scientific expertise cannot dispose of them in a few words as simply later inventions.

In this regard it is well to observe that these facts are not only attested to and narrated by the apostles and disciples of Jesus, but in many cases they are admitted by his opponents. For example, it is very significant that they did not deny the reality of the miracles performed by Jesus, but that they attributed them to the power of Satan....

If we accept the gospel account of Jesus' miracles — and there is no reason not to accept it other than prejudice against the supernatural — one cannot doubt a unique logic which links together all those "signs" and demonstrates their derivation from God's salvific economy. They serve to reveal His love for us — that merciful love which overcomes evil with good — as is shown by the very presence and action of Jesus Christ in the world.

— Pope John Paul II,
Wonders and Signs: The Miracles of Jesus, 13–15, 50

≈ Quiet Time and Then Discussion ≈

Questions for Meditation

1. Did Jesus actually work miracles?
2. Do miracles still happen?
3. Are miracles an integral part of the Gospel? Can we accept the Christ of the Gospels and reject the possibility of miracles?

Prayer

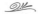

O Lord Jesus Christ, Your very coming to us in this world is the greatest of miracles and was attended by supernatural signs. Throughout Your life and throughout the history of the Church, You have demonstrated Your power and presence by miracles. Finally, in our own time, miracles occur. Give us a belief in these divine signs, which manifest Your power and give Your words the authority of the Son of God. Help us to say, like the centurion, that truly You are "the Son of God." Amen.

Meditation Eleven

Christ, the Source of All Good

READINGS:
John 4: 1–14; Romans 6:1–11; 2 Corinthians 5:11–6:2

The greatest gift that Jesus Christ gave to the human race is the grace of adoption as children of God, by which we are saved. No one can be saved without this gift, which in Latin is called *gratia*, the root of the English word grace. Ordinarily this gift is given at Baptism, and it must be accepted, received, and embraced by anyone with the use of reason. Since no one can consistently lead a virtuous life over a long period of time without grace, we have come to hope and accept in modern times that Christ communicates His gift of grace even to those who have not had an opportunity to hear effectively about Baptism in Christ, or who because of circumstances have never heard the Good News.

No one can believe in the true God, or believe in Christ as Lord and Savior, without having first received a grace of preparation, called in theology prevenient grace (the grace that comes first). This grace does not unite us with God as sons and daughters adopted by Christ, but it is an essential and unmerited impulse or movement that makes it possible for us to accept the gift of faith and salvation. Thus Christ chooses us in God, as Saint Augustine said. We did not choose the Way; the Way chose us. For this reason we must never accept any praise or admiration for our faith. It is always a gift, which was bought for us with the suffering, humiliation, and sacrifice of the Son of God.

Quotation for Meditation

Indeed we also work, but we are only collaborating with God who works, for His mercy has gone before us. It has gone before us so that we may be healed, and follows us so that once healed, we may be given life; it goes before us so that we may be called, and follows us so that we may be glorified; it goes before us so that we may live devoutly, and follows us so that we may always live with God: for without Him we can do nothing.

— Saint Augustine, *De natura et gratia*, cited in the *Catechism of the Catholic Church*, n. 2001

➷ Quiet Time and Then Discussion ➹

Questions for Meditation

1. Why is the grace of God necessary to have eternal life?
2. What does it mean to be an adopted child of God, with Christ as our brother?

Prayer

Lord Jesus Christ, You have sent us the Holy Spirit to give us Your grace, that we may be saved and live in eternal joy with You. We have only to reach out to receive Your grace, and even that reaching out is Your gift. Give us Your Holy Spirit in abundance so that we may be grateful, uncomplaining, and zealous for Your glory and for the salvation of those for whom You lived, died, and rose again. You alone are our Savior. Amen.

Christ, Our Savior, Ascends into Heaven

READINGS:
Matthew 27:18–20; Mark 10:43–45;
Luke 24:13–27; John 10:14–18;
Acts 3:11–26; 4:9–12; Hebrews 2:10–18

In recent years one of the essential and foundational beliefs of Christianity has been obscured in people's minds by skeptical approaches to the study of the Bible and by great mistakes made in understanding human nature by those who produce works of popular psychology. Despite the obvious collapse of a decent law-abiding culture and the rise of media filled with violence, pornography, sexual exploitation, and the abuse of others for pleasure, many people do not realize that we human beings need to be saved. It would seem an obvious fact from what's going on. We need to be saved from ourselves, our weaknesses, our sinful inclinations, and our innate selfishness. In a world so confused and corrupt it is strange that more people do not realize how much they need salvation, although some do realize it. By the grace of God many turn away in disgust from the immorality of our time; others turn not from immorality, but from the hopelessness and despair of a world without love or God.

Particularly at a time of darkness many realize that they have been cheated and misled by the empty worldly culture around them. But that realization is only the beginning. We must turn to Our Savior, to Christ, who alone can save us and who has ascended on high to await our arrival. He saves us by His holy life, which led to His complete sacrifice of obedience and the acceptance of the dangers and limitations of ordinary human existence. When good and evil clash, there must be suffering, and He is lifted up on the Cross to draw us to Himself.

Why does Christ do this? Why did He who was equal to God become a slave and accept death on the Cross? (Philippians 2:1–11). Every day we need to show a loving loyalty to Our Savior who died for us. The act of gratitude for salvation, so dearly bought by Him, will fill us with hope for our world because His love alone can overcome all evil. The last words of Our Savior at His Ascension into heaven are about us and our salvation.

Quotation for Meditation

But the true Mediator, whom in the secret of Your mercy You have shown to men and sent to men, that by His example they might learn humility — the Mediator between God and men, the man Christ Jesus, appeared between sinful mortals and the immortal Just One: for like men He was mortal, like God He was Just; so that, the wages of justice being life and peace, He might, through the union of His own justice with God, make void the death of those sinners whom He justified by choosing to undergo death as they do. He was shown forth to holy men of old that they might be saved by faith in His Passion to come, as we by faith in His Passion now that He has suffered it. As man, He is Mediator; but as Word, He is not something in between, for He is equal to God, God with God, and together one God.

How much Thou hast loved us, O good Father, "Who hast spared not even Thine own Son, but delivered Him up for us wicked men!" How Thou hast loved us, for whom He who "thought it not robbery to be equal with Thee became obedient even unto the death of the Cross," He who alone "was free among the dead, having power to lay down His life and power to take it up again"; for us He was to Thee both Victor and Victim, and Victor because Victim; for us He was to Thee both Priest and Sacrifice, and Priest because Sacrifice; turning us from slaves into Thy sons, by being Thy Son and becoming a slave. Rightly is my hope strong in Him, who sits at Thy right hand and intercedes for us; otherwise I should despair. For many and great are my infirmities, many and great; but Thy medicine is of more power. We might well have thought Thy Word remote from union with man and so have despaired of ourselves, if It had not been "made flesh and dwelt among us."

— Saint Augustine, *Confessions*, X, 43;
See also *Augustine: Major Writings*, 39–40

☙ Quiet Time and Then Discussion ❧

Questions for Meditation

1. Do you think about salvation and what it means to you and those dear to you?
2. At what price is our salvation bought for us by Jesus Christ?

Prayer

Jesus, You alone are my Savior, the one who saves me from everlasting death. You are the Savior of those I love and cherish, although they may not know You or love You. Send Your Holy Spirit to give them the abundant grace of the call to salvation. I pray that they and all the world may turn to You in hope and love. I pray that Your Mother, who is the Mother of our salvation, will prayerfully intercede for us all and especially for those who are away from You. She said at Cana, "Do whatever He tells you." Lord Jesus, pray that at the end of our lives we may follow You in Your great Ascension. Amen.

Meditation Thirteen

Pre-Pentecost Novena

READINGS:
John 14:25–26; John 16:1–15; Acts 1:1–14

One of the providential blessings of the last several decades has been a new awareness by many Christians of the role and importance of the Holy Spirit in our lives. Much of this interest has been occasioned by the Catholic Charismatic Renewal, but it has come from other sources as well, particularly the encyclical *Dominum et Vivificantem* of Pope John Paul II. It is not enough to speak of the Holy Spirit or to pray to Him; we must also allow Him to lead us, speak to and even through us, so that we do His work. This idea often leaves people puzzled. How do I become sensitive to the call and movement of the Holy Spirit?

The best way is to turn to Him wherever we are, even if it is the wrong place. Wherever we are, if we call on the Holy Spirit to help us do good and follow His will, to be true disciples of Jesus, He will lead us on. From that moment we must follow the gospel teachings and try to be as obedient to God's will as we can, even when adversity and trial come upon us. Wherever we are, we can always take the next good step. If we cannot understand what that step should be, we need to pause and pray. The next step will become clear. Even if we err in trying to do the right thing, the Holy Spirit will guide us. There is a saying, "God writes straight with crooked lines." This is the work of the Holy Spirit. The more someone tries to follow the direction of the Holy Spirit, not looking far ahead but being satisfied with one step at a time, the easier it is to follow the way of Christ. The souls who follow Him faithfully often accomplish immense good and achieve great things, even though the malice of the wicked seems to destroy them. In our own time we have seen this with Saints Maximilian Kolbe and Teresa Benedicta of the Cross (Edith Stein), who relied on the Holy Spirit. They died in a man-made hell, and yet they overcame all. Come, Holy Spirit, and lead us.

Quotation for Meditation
The Pillar of the Cloud
JOHN HENRY NEWMAN (1801–1890)

Lead, kindly Light, amid the encircling gloom,
    Lead Thou me on!
The night is dark, and I am far from home —
    Lead Thou me on!
Keep Thou my feet; I do not ask to see
The distant scene — one step enough for me.
I was not ever thus, nor pray'd that Thou
    Shouldst lead me on.
I loved to choose and see my path; but now
    Lead Thou me on!
I loved the garish day, and, spite of fears,
Pride ruled my will; remember not past years.
So long Thy power hath blest me, sure it still
    Will lead me on,
O'er moor and fen, o'er crag and torrent, till
    The night is gone.
And with the morn those angel faces smile
Which I have loved long since, and lost awhile.

Quiet Time and Then Discussion

Questions for Meditation

1. Am I aware of the Holy Spirit in my life?
2. Do I allow Him to lead me?
3. When do I fail to do this?

Prayer

Holy Spirit, come and shed Your divine, life-giving light on the Church, the world, our nation, and each one we care about. Give hope to the hopeless, peace to the distraught, and conversion to those lost along the way. Lift up our hearts that we may be Your witnesses by the way we live and speak, and heal our wounds through Christ Our Lord. Amen.

Pentecost

READINGS:
John 16:1–11; Acts 2:1–36; Galatians 5:22–23

After the Resurrection, the most thrilling event in the New Testament is the coming of the Holy Spirit. We might ask what the history of Christianity would have been like if the Holy Spirit had not come in this startling and remarkable way. The Holy Spirit was always with the apostles in a certain sense, since they were in the state of grace. Pentecost is the celebration of the obvious and undeniable way that Christ's followers are filled with the Holy Spirit. According to Saint Paul, this results in the fruits of the Holy Spirit, which are love, joy, peace, patience, kindness, goodness, faithfulness, gentleness and self-control. The followers of Christ also receive the gifts of the Holy Spirit, which are wisdom, understanding, counsel, knowledge, courage, loyalty and reverence.

In our own times we have seen the fruits of the Holy Spirit in many movements of the Church, including the Charismatic

Renewal, which is explicitly related to Pentecost, and Cursillo, Marriage Encounter, and movements dedicated to Our Lady. It is worth mentioning to members of the Oratory that Saint Catherine of Genoa explicitly referred to the baptism of the Holy Spirit when describing a sudden experience of conversion and enlightenment. The annual liturgical celebration of Pentecost gives us a chance to ask ourselves if we are open to the Holy Spirit and His inspirations.

Do I ask His guidance and am I willing to make the sacrifices to follow the inspiration? We often do not follow the inspirations of the Holy Spirit because they will require sacrifice. The other problem is that we can easily assume that our own pet theories are the voice of the Holy Spirit. For this reason the guidance and governance of the Church, the community of Christ, are necessary to see that we are not just following our own ideas.

Quotation for Meditation
Come Holy Spirit

Come, thou Holy Spirit, come,
and from thy celestial home
shed a ray of light divine!
Come, thou Father of the poor!

Come, thou Source of all our store!
Come, within our bosoms shine!

Thou, of comforters the best;
thou, the soul's most welcome guest;
sweet refreshment here below;
in our labor, rest most sweet;
grateful coolness in the heat;
solace in the midst of woe.

O most blessed Light divine,
shine within these hearts of thine,
and our inmost being fill!
Where thou art not, man hath naught,
nothing good in deed or thought,
nothing free from taint of ill.

Heal our wounds, our strength renew;
on our dryness pour thy dew;
wash the stains of guilt away;
bend the stubborn heart and will;
melt the frozen, warm the chill;
guide the steps that go astray.

On the faithful, who adore
and confess thee, evermore
in thy sevenfold gift descend;

give them virtue's sure reward
give them thy salvation, Lord;
give them joys that never end.

(TRANSLATION BY FATHER EDWARD CASWALL)

❧ Quiet Time and Then Discussion ❧

Questions for Meditation

1. Do I think of the Holy Spirit and His influence in my life?
2. Do I ask for and use His guidance and inspiration?
3. Do I pray seriously every day to the Holy Spirit and ask for His help? Is He as real to me as the Father and the Son?

Prayer

Holy Spirit, come and make Your presence known to me, all who are dear to me, and the whole Church. Give us the peace to recall Your gifts and enjoy the fruits of Your work. Make me, Holy Spirit, Your instrument so that I may be a disciple of Jesus. Amen.

Meditation Fifteen

The Mystery of the Trinity
(Trinity Sunday)

READINGS:
Matthew 28:16–20; 2 Corinthians 1:19–22; John 15:4–11

During the Church year we are asked to contemplate the
mysteries of our redemption especially during the cycle that
begins with Advent, calls to our attention the memorials of Our
Lord's life, and comes to an end with the celebration of the most
Holy Trinity. We invoke the Triune God, as the Trinity is properly called, many times a day — when we make the sign of the
Cross, at the end of the prayers at Mass, and in blessings. But the
doctrine of the Holy Trinity is so mysterious that we seldom
think of what we can know about the infinite reality from which
all things proceed.

Since the time Our Lord spoke of the Father and the Holy
Spirit and identified Himself as the Son of God, Christians, led

by the Church Fathers, have tried to understand what they could from His words in the New Testament. They asked what Christ meant when He spoke of the Father and the Holy Spirit, and of Himself being the Son of God equal to the Father. As the Church emerged from centuries of persecution, it began to study these things. At the Council of Nicea (A.D. 325) the priest Arius was condemned for describing Christ as a lesser God than the Father. The bishops at Nicea, with the approval of the bishop of Rome, declared that there is but one God, in whom there are three persons — in other words, a triple unity, or trinity. Later the First Council of Constantinople (381) made very clear that the Holy Spirit was also "Lord and Giver of life," equal to the Father and the Son.

The Trinity must always remain the deepest of mysteries — the mystery of God Himself — but the councils give us a partial explanation. A person is that which does something, a principle of predication. The Father alone is the origin of all being. The Son is the Word of God and receives from the Father all that the Father gives Him out of love, which is His whole self. The love between Father and Son is equal to them and is therefore yet another Person, the Holy Spirit. This is not an explanation of the Trinity; it is simply the idea of the three divine Persons, who are equal to but distinct from one another, as revealed in the Christian dogma of one God. We learn two very great things from meditating on the Trinity: first, God is infinitely mysterious; second, out of all eternity He is not a solitary Person but a single being filled with relationship and love.

Quotation for Meditation

O Lord our God, we believe in you, Father and Son and Holy Spirit. Truth would not have said, "Go and baptize the nations in the name of the Father and of the Son and of the Holy Spirit" (Matt. 28:19), unless you were a triad. Nor would you have commanded us to be baptized, Lord God, in the name of any who is not Lord God. Nor would it have been said with divine authority, "Hear, O Israel, the LORD your God is one God" (Deut. 6:4), unless while being a triad you were still one Lord God. And if you, God and Father, were yourself also the Son your Word Jesus Christ, were yourself also your gift the Holy Spirit, we would not read in the documents of truth "God sent his Son" (Gal. 4:4), nor would you, only-begotten one, have said of the Holy Spirit, "whom the Father will send in my name" (John 14:26), and, "whom I will send you from the Father" (John 15:26). Directing my attention toward this rule of faith as best I could, as far as you enabled me to, I have sought you and desired to see intellectually what I have believed, and I have argued much and toiled much. O Lord my God, my one hope, listen to me lest out of weariness I should stop wanting to seek you, but let me seek your face always, and with ardor. Do you yourself give me the strength to seek, having caused yourself to be found and having given me the hope of finding you more and more. Before you lies my strength and my weakness; preserve the one, heal the other. Before you lies my knowledge and my ignorance; where you have opened to me, receive me as I come in; where you have shut to me, open to me as I knock. Let me remember you, let me understand you, let me love you. Increase these things in me until you refashion me entirely.

— Saint Augustine, *The Trinity*, XV:51,
from *Works of Saint Augustine*, 436;
See also *Augustine: Major Writings*, 128–129

⊰ Quiet Time and Then Discussion ⊱

Questions for Meditation
1. Do you pray to each Person of the Trinity?
2. Are you aware of the Trinity in your life?

Prayer

Most Holy Trinity, Father, Son, and Holy Spirit, we bow in the most profound worship of the mystery of Your Being. Our beloved Savior revealed this mystery to us, and we accept and rejoice in it. The mystery of eternal love explains why You created the world and human beings to share in Your love and to come at last to the mystery of eternal love through the salvation that the Son and Word of God won for us on the Cross. Amen.

Meditation Sixteen

The Judgment of Christ

READINGS:
Matthew 25:31–46; Matthew 7:12–27;
John 3:16–21; John 14:15–17

In the creed we profess our belief that Jesus Christ, risen from the dead, ascended into heaven, and seated at the right hand of the Father, will come to judge the living and the dead. A few decades ago Christians of all denominations often thought of and prepared for the judgment of Christ. They tried to follow God's law and the way of the Gospel because all would render an account at the time of death. Christ Himself said that He will come with His angels and reward each person according to his deeds (Matthew 16:27). In addition, Our Savior described the Last Judgment in very precise terms in Matthew 25. Almost all the parables of Jesus warn us to be ready for God's judgment.

Much contemporary discussion of what is morally right or permissible almost ignores the fact that we will be judged by

Christ. He did all that was necessary to save us by the greatest love, but He warns us that those who reject His teaching bring a judgment and condemnation on themselves (John 3:16–21). The ultimate reason for this judgment is that God is goodness itself, pure and absolute holiness and justice. Sin is a futile and destructive use of our freedom, time, and energy to do what is opposed to this holiness and justice. Because we have free will, even if it is limited and damaged by original sin, we can go against God's will and the holiness of His being. Ultimately, all sin is an act of idolatry against the first commandment; it puts something in the place of God. It is inevitable that Christ, who gave us forgiveness and grace and the promise of salvation, must separate the good from the bad, the sheep from the goats. This happens once at the hour of death, when we meet Him in all His holiness, truth and love, and again at the mysterious Last Judgment of the world, when God's judgment and truth are known to all who have ever lived. Jesus tells us to be ready. Being ready is what our human life is about.

Quotation for Meditation

One day we too shall be resurrected and placed before the awful white throne. Everything on which we formerly leaned, behind which we formerly hid will disappear. All camouflage, trenches, arms. All earthly guards and allies. All rights, honors, works, successes and anything else that has helped us to avoid the truth. All these will fall away, vanish under the penetrating ray of the Judge. We ourselves shall wonder whether we still really exist. No place will be found for our poor being. The same Power that created us will weigh us to see how much of us actually *is*, for genuine existence is possible only through truth and justice, faith and love; our existence, then, will be appallingly questionable. We shall feel ourselves being undermined by nothingness, sucked down towards the void. Only our naked conscience will stand before God's gaze. May His mercy sustain us in that hour!

— Romano Guardini, *The Lord*, 613–614

⚞ Quiet Time and Then Discussion ⚟

Questions for Meditation

1. Do you sometimes think of the judgment of God?
2. Does this thought have any effect on your life?
3. Do we remind others of the judgment of God when at times they are doing what is wrong?

Prayer

O Lord Jesus Christ, You are truth and holiness. To be in Your presence is like standing near the sun. Help me to prepare for the day when I will be in Your holy and pure presence. Forgive my sins and call me always to a holy life. Help me to see that sin is darkness and evil and that You alone lead the way to eternal life. Amen.

Meditation Seventeen

The Last Judgment

READINGS:
Matthew 3:11–12; John 5:19–29;
Revelation 20:11–21:8

From early times the Church has taught that we are judged at the time of death, and our eternal fate is sealed. There are three possible outcomes: immediate entrance into eternal life, a period of purification, or eternal loss, called damnation. Later we shall consider each of these possibilities in some depth. Because God is justice itself and mercy itself, accounts must be settled with regard to every rational soul. All the world's wrongs must be righted; and before all who have lived, God's justice must be acknowledged and pronounced at the end of the ages.

This does not mean that we earned our eternal salvation, although Saint Paul does call it a prize. Christ Our Lord won for each of us the grace of salvation. However, the wicked have often done much evil and appear by any human calculation to have escaped any sanction. There are also innumerable just and righteous people who have led miserable lives because of injustice and abuse. Just think of all the people in world history who suffered as slaves all their lives. It is the Church's belief, based especially on the Gospels and the mysterious Book of Revelation, that Christ Himself, as the resurrected divine Person, will come and mete out justice for all to see. Then will the crooked ways be made straight and the rough ways smooth. We hardly even think of that judgment, but we need to do so if we want to follow the commandments and obligations given by Christ to His followers.

No one can stand before God in His absolute truth, justice, and goodness without calling on His mercy. We learn that from the confession and repentance of the Good Thief on the cross. We all hope that we too will hear Christ's same words welcoming us to paradise, that is, to eternal life. If life's injustice bothers you, you do not think enough about the Last Judgment. If you find yourself morally drifting, you should try to remember that Christ tells us, "Everyone will be rewarded according to his deeds." When those in public life who are supposed to be leaders of the people are themselves corrupted by the pagan values of our times — like pro-abortion politicians — we must recall that we shall all be judged by God before the whole human race. This future event is very difficult to imagine; that it will happen is beyond question.

Quotation for Meditation

It is hardly an exaggeration to say that also among Christians profound consciousness of the Lord's return has become a rarity. Between preoccupation with the last things and present reality stands the wall known as the scientific viewpoint. But doesn't this entail an essential loss to Christian faith? Christianity has long since taken its place as Christian culture in the world, where it has become an integral part of the whole, and where it is only too inclined to share the general conception of a world to be ended by natural phenomena. Thus Christianity today lacks the tension which lent its early centuries their clear-cut decisiveness, their ardor and *élan*. The fact that most of the early Christians were converted as adults also did much to increase the earnestness and enlightened clarity of their faith. Nevertheless, faith in Christ's coming is not dead, and all faith has a certain seed-like dormancy. It can rest for centuries only suddenly to put forth root and leaf. Perhaps before this can happen, Christianity must lose some of its complacency. The term "Christian culture" must be purged of all that is questionable in it. The gulf between Revelation and the world must reopen. Perhaps a new period of per-

secution and outlawry must come to shake Christians back to a
living consciousness of the values for which they stand. Such a
period might also enliven belief in Christ's coming. It is difficult
to say. Different elements of Christian truth have different seasons. At times they are powerfully felt, at others they recede into
the background, seem to lose their importance and luster, only
to reappear in response to some new vital need.

— Romano Guardini, *The Lord*, 554

⤚ Quiet Time and Then Discussion ⤙

Questions for Meditation

1. Do I ever think that there is injustice in life, that the
   good suffer and the wicked prosper?
2. Do I recall the Last Judgment at these times?
3. Do I think about this judgment as I make my way
   through life?

Prayer

Lord Jesus, You have told us of the great judgment that awaits us and that we should prepare for it every day. Yet we live surrounded by those who seem to be unaware or ignore this judgment. Give us the grace of the Holy Spirit to follow your injunction to "be ready," to walk on the straight path, and to enter by the narrow gate. Amen.

Meditation Eighteen

The Holy Catholic Church

~~©

READINGS:
Matthew 16:13–20; John 21:9–17;
1 Thessalonians 5:12–22; 1 Timothy 3:14–16

Since the first days following the Resurrection, it has been evident in Scripture itself that the community we call the Church has existed. The Scripture readings given above for our consideration are only a small, but significant, sample of quotations that reveal that Christ intended to begin a community that would last until the end of the world. Despite their failure on Holy Thursday and Good Friday, the apostles, having been confirmed by the Holy Spirit, became the first overseers, or bishops (what overseer means) of this Church, or *ecclesia*. (In Greek and Latin, *ecclesia* refers to a congregation, which is translated in English as church.)

Christ gave these apostle-overseers the power to forgive sins, to celebrate the mysterious Eucharist, to baptize, and heal the sick. As the New Testament moved on past the time of the Gospels, we see Saint Paul giving advice to Church members and leaders, especially in what are called the pastoral epistles — 1 and 2 Timothy, and Titus. We see the life of the Church developing in all the epistles, including those of Peter, John, James, and Jude. The author of the Book of Revelation has warnings and messages for various specific churches in different locations.

In the sixteenth century, when the Church was weakened by such calamities as the Black Death and the Hundred Years' War, some devout Catholics decided to abandon the Church with all its ills and establish a new community, based on their reading of the New Testament. This was a church without bishops or priests, without any sacraments except Baptism. These people were first called Anabaptists. The community they founded, however, was not at all like the early Church, which possessed not only Baptism but also the apostolic teaching authority and the other sacraments. Even Luther and Calvin, who never meant to start a new church, claimed that they kept the teachings and institutions of the early Church. Actually, they added new doctrines like predestination and omitted the teaching on the Eucharist as a representation of the sacrificial death of Christ.

With all the ills of the Church during that time, we should not judge those who left it, because we do not know what we would have done if we had been in their situation. Many saintly Catholics — Catherine and Bernardine of Siena, Ignatius of Loyola, Teresa of Avila, and John of the Cross — joined the rising call for reform within the Church, begun in part by Saint Catherine of Genoa, who died before Luther's departure from the Church. The fact is that Christ had prophesied that the powers of hell would attack the Church but that they would not prevail. We see the same thing happening around us right now. This is a time to be faithful to Christ and, because of this fidelity, to be loyal to the Church He founded.

Quotations for Meditation
Saint Augustine on the Church

Hold this fast and keep it entirely fixed in your memory, as children of the Church's training and of the Catholic Faith, that you may perceive Christ to be the Head and the Body, and the same Christ to be also the Word of God, the Only-begotten, equal to the Father, and so may see how great is the grace whereby you pertain to God, that He, Who is one with the Father, has willed to be one with us…. Christ and the Church are two in one flesh. The "two" you must refer to the distance of His Majesty from us.

Clearly there are two. For we are not also the Word; we are not also God in the beginning with God: we are not also He by Whom all things were made (John 1:1–3).

> — Commentary on Psalm 142,
> as cited in *An Augustine Synthesis*, 215–216

The whole Christ is Head and Body, which truth I doubt not you know well: the Head is our Saviour Himself.... But His body is the Church, not this one or that, but spread throughout the whole world. Nor is it only that which now is among men who are living in the present life, but it is in those belonging to it who have been before us and in those who are to come after us, even unto the end of the world. For the whole Church, which consists of all the faithful, since all the faithful are members of Christ, hath that Head set in heaven, and it governeth His body. And although it is separated from our vision, yet is it joined together in charity. Hence the whole Christ is Head and its body.

> — Commentary on Psalm 56,
> as cited in *An Augustine Synthesis*, 218

∽ Quiet Time and Then Discussion ∽

Questions for Meditation

1. Have the present scandals eroded my faith in the Church?
2. Should any scandal really affect my faith?
3. How do I help others whose faith has been weakened?

Prayer

Lord Jesus, at the very time of Your betrayal and death, You appointed the apostles to take Your place, to feed and shepherd Your sheep. Many pages of Church history are filled with souls of great holiness, but other pages are dark and shocking, like Good Friday. Give us all the grace through the Holy Spirit to love and serve Your Church, which according to Saint Paul is Your mysterious and spiritual body. Amen.

Meditation Nineteen

The Church and the Sacraments

READINGS:
Matthew 26:26–29; Mark 14:22–25; Luke 22:14–20;
John 6:32–40; 1 Corinthians 11:17–30

The Holy Eucharist, the other sacraments, and the New Testament are the greatest treasures of the Catholic Church. Together they justify the Church's existence and provide the strongest reason why we must remain faithful to the Church in good times and in bad. Although Baptism should always be given as the bath of redemption, it is also the initiation into Church membership, the incorporation into Christ. Nevertheless, the grace of baptism can be conferred apart from the Church, as we know. So can the sacrament of marriage, although both of these sacraments properly belong to the life of the Church. However, the other sacraments can be shared only in the Catholic Church or in the Orthodox Churches, which have a special sacramental relationship with each other, since they have a valid priesthood and by their very nature should be more united than they are at present.

The sacraments, which are called the divine mysteries in the Eastern Church, actually bring Christ to minister to us, His people. He is the one who really baptizes and confirms, who gives His flesh to eat and takes away our sins. He is the one who strengthens the sick and prepares the dying. He ordains the bishops, priests, and deacons, and He blesses the marriage and makes it a sacrament, uniting the couple in Himself. The sacraments are so necessary that even a priest who is excommunicated, if he is present when someone is dying, can legitimately administer the sacraments.

Pope John Paul II stressed the fact that the Church itself flows from the Holy Eucharist. We shall consider this truth in our next meditation. The mystical reality of Christ's presence with us, the re-presentation of His sacrificial death, and His nourishment of us by the grace of Holy Communion are three gifts from Our Savior. What an astounding motive for prayerful gratitude we have in the Eucharist and in all the sacraments! We will spend several weeks on the sacraments in our later meditations. Now we rejoice in the fact that one of the principal reasons for the Church is that through it rivers of life flow to us from Christ in the sacraments.

Quotation for Meditation

The sacraments are "of the Church" in the double sense that they are "by her" and "for her." They are "by the Church," for she is the sacrament of Christ's action at work in her through the mission of the Holy Spirit. They are "for the Church" in the sense that "the sacraments make the Church,"[5] since they manifest and communicate to men, above all in the Eucharist, the mystery of communion with the God who is love, One in three persons.

Forming "as it were, one mystical person" with Christ the head, the Church acts in the sacraments as "an organically structured priestly community."[6] Through Baptism and Confirmation the priestly people is enabled to celebrate the liturgy, while those of the faithful "who have received Holy Orders, are appointed to nourish the Church with the word and grace of God in the name of Christ."[7]

The ordained ministry or *ministerial* priesthood is at the service of the baptismal priesthood.[8] The ordained priesthood guarantees that it really is Christ who acts in the sacraments through the Holy Spirit for the Church. The saving mission entrusted by the Father to his incarnate Son was committed to the apostles and through them to their successors: they receive the Spirit of Jesus to act in his name and in his person.[9] The ordained minister is the sacramental bond that ties the liturgical action to what the apostles said and did and, through them, to the words and actions of Christ, the source and foundation of the sacraments.

— *Catechism of the Catholic Church*, nn. 1118–1120

ᴥ Quiet Time and Then Discussion ᴥ

Questions for Meditation

1. What would I be missing if I had not been given the grace of the Catholic faith?
2. How does the Holy Eucharist instituted by Christ give rise to the Church?
3. Can we ever receive Holy Communion completely worthily, or should we always experience it with some sense of repentance?

Prayer

Lord Jesus, You promised to be with us until the end of the world. How grateful we should be. How astonishing that You are with us, to serve us and care for us! Help me in my life to grow each day in love for the Church, which brings us the bread of life. Amen.

Meditation Twenty

The Church from the Eucharist

READINGS:
Hebrews 8:1–7; 9:11–28; 1 Corinthians 11:23–34;
Philippians 2:5–11

In the encyclical *Ecclesia de Eucharistia* (The Church from the Eucharist) (2003), Pope John Paul II takes up the beautiful relationship between the Holy Eucharist and the Church. This is not an easy idea to comprehend, but it is one that can give great meaning to the individual's spiritual life. Every day we are invited to share in the Paschal Mystery, the loving and obedient sacrifice of the Son of God, born into this world as the child of Mary and our brother. In this mystery He offers Himself to the Father as the paschal lamb, the little creature sacrificed so that its blood could save the children of God in Egypt from death.

Christ offered Himself on the Cross, but the Church, based on Saint Paul (1 Corinthians 11:23–34) and the tradition of very early times, teaches us that He continues to offer Himself in what is called the Paschal Mystery. Most Catholics do not think of their lives united to the Paschal Mystery, but that participation, total and mysterious, will be our eternal life in heaven. The Mass here on earth begins our eternal life. If we begin to think of the Paschal Mystery, our personal life can be transformed; our view of the Church, as it really is in God's eyes, can be transformed as well.

Quotation for Meditation

The Church was born of the Paschal Mystery. For this very reason the Eucharist, which is in an outstanding way the sacrament of the Paschal Mystery, stands at the center of the Church's life. This is already clear from the earliest images of the Church found in the Acts of the Apostles: "They devoted themselves to the Apostles' teaching and fellowship, to the breaking of bread and the prayers" (2:42). The "breaking of the bread" refers to the Eucharist. Two thousand years later we continue to relive that primordial image of the Church. At every celebration of the Eucharist we are spiritually brought back to the Paschal Triduum: to the events of the evening of Holy Thursday, to the Last Supper and to what followed it. The institution of the Eucharist sacramentally anticipated the events which were about to take place, beginning with the agony in Gethsemane. Once again we see Jesus as He leaves the Upper Room, descends with His disciples to the Kidron valley and goes to the Garden of Olives. Even today that garden shelters some very ancient olive trees. Perhaps they witnessed what happened beneath their shade that evening, when Christ in prayer was filled with anguish "and His sweat became like drops of blood falling down upon the ground" (cf. Luke 22:44). The blood which shortly before He had given to the Church as the drink of salvation in the sacrament of the Eucharist, began to be shed; its outpouring would then be completed on Golgotha to become the means of our redemption: "Christ … as high priest of the good things to come … entered once for all into the Holy Place, taking not the blood of goats and calves but His own blood, thus securing an eternal redemption" (Hebrews 9:11–12).

The hour of our redemption. Although deeply troubled, Jesus does not flee before His "hour." "And what shall I say? 'Father, save me from this hour'? No, for this purpose I have come to this hour" (John 12:27). He wanted His disciples to keep Him company, yet He had to experience loneliness and abandonment: "So, could you not watch with me one hour? Watch and pray that you may not enter into temptation" (Matthew 26:40–41). Only John would remain at the foot of the

Cross, at the side of Mary and the faithful women. The agony in Gethsemane was the introduction to the agony of the Cross on Good Friday. The holy hour, the hour of the redemption of the world. Whenever the Eucharist is celebrated at the tomb of Jesus in Jerusalem, there is an almost tangible return to His "hour," the hour of His Cross and glorification. Every priest who celebrates Holy Mass, together with the Christian community which takes part in it, is led back in spirit to that place and that hour.

— *Ecclesia de Eucharistia*, 3, 4

⊸⊱ Quiet Time and Then Discussion ⊰⊷

Questions for Meditation

1. Do I think of my life united with Christ in His suffering and death?
2. Do I have a renewed view of the Church as our entrance into the Paschal Mystery?
3. Do I think of each day as part of Christ's offering to the Holy Trinity?

Prayer

O Lord Jesus Christ, You came into this world to be our priest. Because of the sins of human beings, You suffered bitterly and offered Your life in obedience on the Cross. You have called each one of us to carry Your Cross. Help us now to see that the carrying of that Cross envelops us in the immense mystery of divine love, which You showed to the Father as You accepted suffering and death peacefully on the Cross. Help us to have a spirit of sacrifice. Amen.

Meditation Twenty-One

The Holy Catholic Church:
Apostles, Bishops, Priests, and Deacons

~~❧~~

READINGS:
Matthew 16:13–20; 1 Timothy 3:1–13; 4:14–16;
5:17–25; Titus 1:5–9

A thoughtful reading of the Gospels will reveal several distinct groups of people who were part of Our Lord's life. It is clear that He assigned them various roles to play in His work of salvation. He identified this divine work when He said that He had come "to save the world" (John 12:47).

The first group are His closest followers, to whom He entrusted the task of "feeding the lambs and sheep" and of bringing the Good News to the end of the world. He entrusted them with the works of salvation on His behalf. Among the works are the baptism of the nations, the offering of the Eucharist "in His memory" (or prayer of thanksgiving with the mysterious designation of the bread and wine as His body and blood), and the forgiveness of sins. He called these men His apostles. Others, the disciples, were to bring His word and power to cure illnesses and to cast out evil spirits.

There are other groups as well, the most notable of whom are His family and the women who followed Him from Galilee and stood by the Cross.

There were the multitudes who believed in Him. We see them so often, but not as a well-defined group like the apostles and the disciples. They are often referred to as those who listened to His word, believed in Him, welcomed Him on Palm Sunday, and were present at the first Pentecost. There are also the larger multitudes, for whom He had compassion because they were like sheep without a shepherd.

There are other categories too, although they are not groups: those who see His signs but reject them and Him, those who have ears but do not hear, and finally His enemies, for whom He prays on the Cross.

The first and most obviously defined group are the twelve men Christ sends out to be His representatives. We are given their names, and we see them constantly throughout the Gospels. Our Lord teaches them, gives them instruction, which He does not share with others. He corrects them, appears to be disappointed in them, sends them, calls them His friends in the most affectionate way at the Last Supper, returns to them after the Resurrection, and sends them out to the ends of the world. Who took the place of these first collaborators, or apostles? Who increased their ranks as the new faith began to spread to the ends of the world?

The Greek word for those who were added to the ranks of the apostles means overseers. Changing the Greek words into Latin, we get *epi* (over) and *scopos* (look or see), which gives us the Latin word *episcopus* — in English, bishop. Saint Paul often speaks of the bishop overseers, who fulfilled the tasks of the apostles, and he writes to two of them, Timothy and Titus. They were among the first bishops of the Church.

Saint Paul also makes a distinction between those he leaves in charge (overseers) and the elders (see Titus 1:5–9). The Greek word for elder is translated in Latin as *presbyter*, from which we get the English word priest. In the earliest tradition of all ancient churches — Catholic, Orthodox and apostolic, like the Armenian and Coptic churches — these distinct groups of ordained men have been defined in the same way. They were designated at the end of the first century by Saint Clement, Bishop of Rome (died A.D. 94) and at the beginning of the second century by Saint Ignatius, Bishop of Antioch (died 106). To the bishops and priests were added the deacons, which we find in the Acts of the Apostles 6:1–6.

It is strange that many devout Gospel-loving Christians don't see these distinct groups of people singled out by the original apostles in the laying on of hands and prayer (see Acts 6:6 for one of several references to what we now call ordination.) Presumably those who give special importance to the King James version of the Bible would be astonished to find that those who made that translation had the title of bishops and priests of the Anglican Church. Moreover, they saw themselves as Catholic clergy, although separated from the Bishop of Rome because of the order of the King of England.

Bishops, priests, and deacons are not supermen. Like the apostles, they can sin, fall away, and even betray Christ, as the apostle Judas did. Good bishops, priests, and deacons do their work to feed and guard the flock of God; they are filled with an awareness that when Christ selected the man to lead the apostles, He chose the only person recorded to have confessed to Jesus Christ that he was a sinful man.

Quotation for Meditation

"Christ, make me become and remain the servant of your unique power, the servant of your sweet power, the servant of your power that knows no eventide. Make me a servant. Indeed the servant of your servants.

"Be not afraid to welcome Christ and accept His power. Help the Pope and all those who wish to serve Christ and with Christ's power to serve the human person the whole of mankind.

"Be not afraid. Open wide the doors for Christ. To his saving power open the boundaries of states, economic and political systems, the vast fields of culture, civilization, and development.

"Be not afraid. Christ knows "what is in man." He alone knows it....

"I ask you ... I beg you, let Christ speak to [you]. He alone has the words of life, yes, of eternal life."

— Words of Pope John Paul II to the Catholic world
on the day of his election as Pope,
cited in *Witness to Hope*, 262

❧ Quiet Time and Then Discussion ❧

Questions for Meditation

1. Am I as aware as I should be that Christ established the office of bishop and that priests and deacons have assisted in this holy order since the time of the apostles?

2. With all the attacks of the media and the revelation of the moral failure of some bishops and priests, has my faith in what Christ did become clouded?

3. Do I react appropriately when the Pope, bishops, and priests are attacked in the media? Do I protest, or do I give my consent to this by silence?

Prayer

Come, Holy Spirit, and renew Your Church. Help each of us — clergy, religious, and laity — to respect the Holy Orders that You bestow as part of Christ's plan of salvation. Help those called to be bishops, priests, and deacons to fulfill their office well; guide us in supporting them as those sent by Christ. Amen.

Meditation Twenty-Two

The Marks of the Church

READINGS:
Matthew 16:18–19; Ephesians 4:1–6;
1 Corinthians 12:1–31

Generations of youngsters studying the *Catechism* learned that the Catholic Church has four distinguishing marks, or characteristics. They are historical signs that distinguished it as the Church established by Christ. The Church was said to be one, holy, catholic, and apostolic. We accepted these qualities of the Church as both obvious and as static or permanent signs. That was it. Later, as religious education tended to be more ecumenical — some might say less triumphalistic and, in some cases, less informed — these marks of the Church were seldom taught. This is unfortunate, since they are succinct ways of describing the Church.

I think the marks of the Church should be seen in a dynamic way rather than as a static possession, like favors from God in a treasure box. By "dynamic" I mean that they are qualities the Church must constantly strive toward. Their continuous existence is ultimately made possible only by the grace of the Holy Spirit, using the cooperative wills of those members of the Church who respond to His grace.

Let us look at unity. Throughout Church history there has been a constant struggle to preserve the doctrinal unity of the Church. This means that we believe something and that we act as though we believe it. We profess one Lord, one faith, one baptism, functioning together as disciples of the One Lord Jesus Christ, in union with the bishops, especially the bishop who succeeded Peter as the head of the apostolic band. The faith is there, but we must not presume. In the confusing sea of human thought, unity exists in a constant struggle with the rebelliousness of the human heart. Baptism must be believed in and practiced as Christ meant it to be, as a sign of unity. Struggle is necessary because the Church on earth does not exist in books, declarations, or rituals. It exists in the hearts and souls of the faithful. If we follow the Gospel teachings of Christ and the tradition of the apostles, as interpreted by the Church Fathers, we are the living stones with which God builds His Church.

This dynamism, this struggle, is even more obvious if we speak of the Church's holiness. Holiness means dedication to living in imitation of the life of Christ, given to us in sanctifying grace. Even in the worst periods of history there were saints, later acknowledged as great saints in the Church. During the dreadful century before the Protestant Reformation, one of the darkest moments in Church history, there was at least one person born every year who would be a canonized saint, like Catherine of Genoa, Teresa of Avila, John of the Cross, and Ignatius Loyola.

The Church is catholic, or universal, only because we try to resist the things that would and could rupture its unity. In the past these evil forces of dissolution included slavery, war, military occupation, and even use of the Church as a source of power and political influence. Today the introduction into the Church of conflict that puts stress on its unity must be resisted, or parts of the Church will become severed from the living body of Christ and even very sincere people will fall into schism or heresy.

Finally, we must always know, follow, and struggle to keep and apply the teaching of the apostles, planted in our hearts and minds by Christ. To be apostolic is to be zealous, brave, and dedicated not to our own comfort and welfare, but to bringing the love of Christ to others, being loyal to Christ in the circumstances of our own lives.

The marks of the Church flow from the Holy Spirit. They are dynamic features of His loving presence, grace, and action among us. We Catholics struggling to live out our Christian vocation in the Church that Christ founded must, according to Pope John Paul II, find strength, energy, and inspiration in the Holy Eucharist. Then the four marks of the Church will not be seen as logos or trademarks; they will be marvelous signs of the Holy Spirit, working in living souls who really make up the Church, the Mystical Body of Christ.

Quotation for Meditation

"This is the sole Church of Christ, which in the Creed we profess to be one, holy, catholic, and apostolic."[10] These four characteristics, inseparably linked with each other,[11] indicate essential features of the Church and her mission. The Church does not possess them of herself; it is Christ who, through the Holy Spirit, makes his Church one, holy, catholic, and apostolic, and it is he who calls her to realize each of these qualities.

Only faith can recognize that the Church possesses these properties from her divine source. But their historical manifestations are signs that also speak clearly to human reason. As the First Vatican Council noted, the "Church herself, with her marvelous propagation, eminent holiness, and inexhaustible fruitfulness in everything good, her catholic unity and invincible stability, is a great and perpetual motive of credibility and an irrefutable witness of her divine mission."[12]

— *Catechism of the Catholic Church*, nn. 811, 812

⟨⟩ Quiet Time and Then Discussion ⟨⟩

Questions for Meditation

1. Was I ever aware of the four marks of the Church?
2. Do I think of myself as called to be a living stone functioning as a dynamic part of the body of Christ?
3. How can I respond to the four marks of the Church, as these unbelieving times seem to sweep over the Church?

Prayer

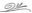

My Savior and Shepherd of my soul, I am deeply troubled by confusion, doubt, lack of loyalty, and false teaching and controversy within the Church. I want to stand with You. I want to encourage unity and peace. I want to grow in holiness and be an informed, willing, witnessing member of the Church. I want those I love to be the same. Please help us, O Lord, as You helped Our Lady and Mary Magdalene, Peter and Paul, Thomas and John, all so different, yet all called to be Your living stones. Amen.

Meditation Twenty-Three

Serving the Church

READINGS:
2 Corinthians 8:16–21; 1 Thessalonians 5:12–28;
Colossians 4:8–18

One of the obligations for members of the Oratory of Divine Love was to serve the Church. Besides attending prayer meetings, members were expected to do works of charity for the poor and needy, give good example of reverence and prayer at Church, and work for the Church.

Here we turn our attention to our obligation to work for the Church. Everyone knows that the Catholic Church in the English-speaking world is in trouble. There are alarming signs of decline on all sides: lack of discipline and silly tinkering with the liturgy, the scandal of the clergy, the decline and impending collapse of what were once thriving religious orders, loss of faith among many, and the disappointing performance of Catholic education. In fact, that is why we refounded the Oratories of Divine Love in the United States.

When Saint Catherine of Genoa and Ettore Vernazza started the Oratory in 1497, it was one of the darkest moments in Church history. Early members of the Oratory did not waste time lamenting; they set to work. They undertook the spiritual and physical care of the sick, especially plague victims by the thousands, and they worked in religious education, which was just beginning as a formal discipline. They catechized both children and adults, some of whom knew little of the faith other than superstition. When parish priests welcomed them, they worked at every task, beginning what we call today voluntarism. When a parish did not welcome them, they went on to the next or to another apostolate where they were welcomed. Their teaching was always orthodox, realistic, and deeply devout, values reflected in Saint Catherine's life. Members of the Oratory were concerned with their own spiritual lives and those of others. Catherine's *Spiritual Dialogue* is a catechism of the struggles and battles of the spiritual journey.[13]

What can Oratorians do today? Look for any kind of Church work you will be able to do well and in accord with the mind of the Church. This might be in your own parish or with some endeavor near where you live or work. It can be a simple, humble task done well for God's love: helping to clean the church, preparing the bulletin, being a minister of the sacraments to the sick, or an usher. It can also be more complicated and time-consuming. Religious education, with all the necessary preparation, is, to my way of thinking, the best use of your time, if you can do it and it is available to you.

There are lots of activities related to what we used to call Catholic Action. For example, pro-life activities of many kinds, working with immigrants who need to be welcomed and assisted, welcoming new parishioners, ecumenical activities, assisting the parish with wedding preparations and funerals, visiting the sick, and especially bringing them the Blessed Sacrament. Where does it all stop? It doesn't. It goes on, according to Our Lord, until the end of the world.

There are many ways of helping the Church, whether through organizations or in silent, unnoticed activities. They are right in front of you, but perhaps you have not seen them. We must always do these things out of love, disinterested love. That means trying to do them with all your heart and with great care and not looking for any personal reward. Outside my little office in the garage there is a sign with Mother Teresa's words: DO NO GREAT THINGS, ONLY SMALL THINGS WITH GREAT LOVE. That says it all.

Quotation for Meditation

The following quotation is taken from the stirring account of Cardinal Nguyễn Văn Thuận of Vietnam. It is part of the description of his imprisonment by the Communist government. Anyone interested in growing spiritually would do well to read the whole book.

During my voyage toward North Vietnam, I was put in chains three times with a man who was non-Catholic, a member of the parliament, and someone known for his fundamentalist Buddhism. Yet, being together in the same terrible situation touched his heart. Later I learned that after his liberation, he willingly related how he had felt honored to be chained with me and had, in fact, always tried to be chained with me, and that we had become friends.

On the ship and afterward in the re-education camp, I had occasion to dialogue with the most varied people: ministers, members of parliament, high civil and military figures, as well as religious authorities among the Cao Đài, Hoà Hảo, Buddhists, Brahmanists, Moslems, and people of different Protestant denominations including Baptists and Methodists. In the camp I was elected bursar, which gave me the responsibility of serving everyone, distributing the food, getting the hot water, and carrying on my back the coal to keep us warm during the night. All this because the other prisoners considered me a man worthy of trust.

Upon my departure from Saigon, Jesus, crucified outside the walls of Jerusalem, made me understand that I had to engage in a new form of evangelization. I no longer acted as a bishop within a diocese, but *extra muros*; as a missionary *ad extra*, *ad vitam*, *ad summum* — going outside, for all my life, to the very limits of my capacity to love and give of myself. Now, yet another dimension opened itself, *ad omnes* — for all.

In the obscurity of faith, in service and in humiliation, the light of hope had changed my vision. I understood that at this point, on this ship, in this prison, was my most beautiful cathedral, and that these prisoners, without exception, were the people of God entrusted to my pastoral care. My prison was divine providence. It was the will of God.

I spoke of all of this to the other Catholic prisoners, and there was born among us a profound communion, a new commitment. We were called to be together *witnesses of hope* for all people.

— Francis Xavier Nguyễn Văn Thuận,
Testimony of Hope, 78–79

꧁ Quiet Time and Then Discussion ꧂

Questions for Meditation

1. What am I actually doing for the Church?
2. What more could I do?
3. What should I do when some activities seem not to be in harmony with the mind of the Church?
4. Can I change others, or should I leave them and work for change somewhere else?

Prayer

O Lord Jesus Christ, You have called us to serve You in our brothers and sisters. This is especially true in the Church, but it extends to all those who are potential members of the Church and all those You have called to eternal salvation by Your death on the Cross. Give me the grace to serve Your Church and, by serving the Church, to make myself available to all my brothers and sisters in the human race, even those who see themselves as my enemies and the enemies of the Church. Amen.

Meditation Twenty-Four

Giving Good Example in Church

✦

READINGS:
Psalm 122; Luke 19:45–46; Matthew 18:20

Apparently things had become rather irreverent at the end of
the fifteenth century, since the Oratory rule calls for members to give a good example of prayerful attention at worship.
Unfortunately, we can observe a widespread lack of reverence in
the Church today.

Reverence is part of human nature. We find varied sincere and
moving acts of reverence in all world religions and cultures.
Declining cultures seem to be the most irreverent; persecuted religions seem to be the most reverent. Reverence is a prayerful sense
of awe and humility, demonstrated by those who experience what
they believe to be the divine presence. There is something almost
mystical about reverence, even when shown by a child. In different ways we are aware of being in the presence of God or of holy

beings who are now with God, like angels and saints. This can occur through personal conviction, an experience of other reverent people around us, and the invitations of grace. Reverence takes us out of our own world, with its petty concerns, and places us in God's presence. At the same time it removes us from trivial and aggravating human needs, and it replaces busy preoccupation with a calm awareness of the beauty and nobility of the human soul.

Reverence draws us away from relating exclusively to our own needs, whether they are the normal experiences felt in childhood or the immature needs of a narcissistic, self-centered adult. Reverence and respect are different realities, but they are related. Following Calvin, the Puritans and their descendants thought of Christ as being very distant, "in a far country," although He could be invoked in prayer and the soul could contact Him. They could even receive His body and blood by a prayerful reception of the bread and wine offered at the Protestant communion service. Thus our image of Calvinist worship is that it was more respectful than reverent.

On the other hand, the Divine Liturgy of the Eastern Church evokes a sense of awe at Christ's mysterious presence in the liturgical prayers and especially in the Eucharistic sacrifice — not that there is a lack of respect, but reverence is much more in focus. In the East, where the liturgical services may be very long, it is not considered disrespectful to attend only part of the liturgy. Such an approach would be incomprehensible in old New England with its respectful Calvinist attitudes.

Unfortunately, Catholic participation in Mass, or liturgy, has two glaring problems. The first is that many view attendance at Mass simply as the fulfillment of the obligation to observe the third commandment. Some seem to come only to get a chore done, arriving late and leaving early. Even the priest may get caught up in this superficial approach to things, rushing through the Mass, oblivious of the fact that while he may show respect, he shows little or no reverence and awe. The other problem with Catholic worship is that it is often an event, a happening. Various activities have the congregation as their focus, not the worship of God. It is obviously essential that the Mass be an inspiration and opportunity for the whole congregation, led by bishops, priests, and deacons, to offer joint worship to God. Mass is not a meditation, but a liturgical action. In these days when people tinker with the liturgy to make it more relevant, or aesthetically attractive, we have lost sight of the highest purposes of the liturgy. We attend Mass in order to join body, soul, heart, and mind with Christ, who makes the eternal offering of Himself to the Godhead, the most holy Trinity. Above all, we should summon every bit of reverence we can. Carefully placed moments of deep silence and fervent interior prayer are part of reverence at Mass. These are our response of awe. The Holy Father says we should be astounded by the Eucharist. Christ actually comes body, blood, soul, and divinity to be with us.

There are many ways to express reverence, including silence, before, during, and after Mass. Oratorians should be working to restore that silence. They should show reverent posture when standing, kneeling, or sitting, giving attention to the action of the Mass and fervent responses to prayers. If people around you are being irreverent, they can learn from your example. Don't be afraid to ask them to be quiet so you can pray. Tell them it's impolite to chat in church — and it is. Walk to and from Communion with a sense of deep reverence. Kneel before and after Mass, and to receive Communion, where it is permitted. Reverence and irreverence are both contagious through the way we dress, act, walk, and generally behave in church. The recent phenomenon of clapping in church lends, I think, a secular attitude of entertainment to liturgy that is most inappropriate. Let us, instead, make a joyful sound to the Lord by our prayer and singing. An Oratorian should be happy to be reverent and recollected at Mass and in church and in that way to give honor to God and good example to others. To use the words of that most reverent Christian, Mother Teresa, give something beautiful to God.

Quotation for Meditation

The following is taken from one of the rules of an Oratory in Genoa, which was obviously only for men. There were also Oratories for women. It speaks also of a prior, who was really the coordinator and held the office only for six months. This is from chapter 10: "Concerning good customs."

Your fraternity cannot include men who either publicly or secretly lead an evil life, namely, a life of concubinage, usury, injustice, blasphemy, and let no one among you gamble, nor stay to watch dice or cards, nor other prohibited games, nor at other licit ones through cupidity; and when in church divine offices are being sung, let no one of you go walking up and down or seek occasion to converse with each other more than is necessary in holy and honest places, always giving good example to each other and to whomever may see you…. Let each in order to form good habits fast one day a week as he is able … Let the appointed feasts be spent in spiritual labors, for they are ordained to this end. The other days let each hear Mass when he is able, or at least be present at the Elevation. The day that the brothers congregate let each brother as he enters the oratory, as he goes to seat himself, say "*Pax vobiscum*" [Peace be with you].

— John Olin, *The Catholic Reformation: Savonarola to Ignatius Loyola*, 22–23

Quiet Time and Then Discussion

Questions for Meditation

1. Do you think there could be improvement in reverence in your parish church?
2. What exactly could be improved?
3. How can you make a difference?

Prayer

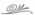

O Lord Jesus Christ, You are our eternal High Priest. Not only do we pray to You but You pray within us. You are the prayer in our midst. Help us to use mind, heart, body, and soul to offer a worthy sacrifice of praise to You and, with You, to the Father. Help us to give the best possible example of joyful and fervent worship to the Lord. Amen.

Meditation Twenty-Five

The Communion of Saints

READINGS:
Acts 2:42–47; 1 Corinthians 12:13–26

Perhaps no words in the Creed mean less to the average Catholic than "I believe in the communion of saints." But when you understand these words, you see that they can mean much for your spiritual life. Communion means sharing good things, especially nourishment and other things necessary for life. Christ is the Head of this spiritual communion of His grace and blessings for salvation. He shares the riches of His grace through the sacraments. The Holy Spirit also governs and guides the whole Church as well as its individual members. The divine gifts engender good things like charity, the teaching of faith, and the example of hope. There are the blessings we receive and share with other members of the Church and with people of good will, especially other Christians, who are closely related to the Church by grace in their souls.

This communion has three states of being: the heavenly Church, the Church of the holy souls on their way to the heavenly Church (or the Church being purified), and the Church on earth. The Church on earth is often called the Church militant because we are engaged in the struggle against sin and evil. Here we consider the heavenly Church, where we all hope to be one day. This is a reality which "eye has not seen, nor ear heard," nor can we think of it in adequate terms. The best description comes from Christ's beautiful but simple expression: "My Father's house." There is also the fascinating and mysterious description in the Book of Revelation, chapters 19 through 22. Perhaps the most important thing for us to remember about the heavenly Church is that the saints are our brothers and sisters and that by their prayers they assist us in our spiritual and material needs. Our Blessed Mother, Queen of all Saints, leads the intercession for us. We also learn from the saints that if they are friends to us, who are struggling souls on earth, we should be friends to one another.

Quotations for Meditation

[A]ll in various ways and degrees are in communion in the same charity of God and neighbor and all sing the same hymn of glory to our God. For all who are in Christ, having His Spirit,

form one Church and cleave together in Him.[14] Therefore the
union of the wayfarers with the brethren who have gone to sleep
in the peace of Christ is not in the least weakened or interrupted,
but on the contrary, according to the perpetual faith of the
Church, is strengthened by communication of spiritual goods.
For by reason of the fact that those in heaven are more closely
united with Christ, they establish the whole Church more firmly
in holiness … [T]hey do not cease to intercede with the Father
for us, showing forth the merits which they won on earth
through the one Mediator between God and man.…[15] Thus by
their brotherly interest our weakness is greatly strengthened.

— *Lumen Gentium*, 49;
See also *Catechism of the Catholic Church*, nn. 954–956

"Do not weep, for I shall be more useful to you after my death
and I shall help you then more effectively than during my life."[16]
"I want to spend my heaven in doing good on earth."[17]
— *Catechism of the Catholic Church*, n. 956

≈ Quiet Time and Then Discussion ≈

Questions for Meditation

1. Do you think occasionally of the saints in heaven and the help they have given us?
2. Do you ever study the lives of the saints to learn from them?
3. Are there any saintly souls around us in this life?

Prayer

O Lord Jesus Christ, You are the King of all Saints of heaven and of earth. Through Your Mystical Body, the Church, we share in Your grace and glory. Help us to be Your instruments to bring Your salvation to others and to live by Your holy words. Amen.

The Church Being Purified

⁓⦉

READINGS:
2 Maccabees 12:45; 1 Corinthians 3:10–15

From early times, Christians have prayed for the dead and have considered those souls passing through a purification on their journey to God's eternal kingdom as part of the great communion of saints. We have prayed for them and asked them to pray for us. All the ancient churches, like the Armenian and Coptic Churches and Saint Thomas Church of India, pray for the dead, as do the Orthodox Churches, which became separated much later. This means that the vast majority of Christians pray for the dead, as do most of the other major world religions.

Originally, the Protestant reformers opposed prayers for the dead. Many of them believed that salvation was decided before you were born and had no relation to your deeds. In Saint Matthew's Gospel (12:31–32), Our Lord indicates that there are sins forgiven in this world and sins "forgiven in the age to come." Perhaps if the Protestant reformers had known of the very early gravestones that showed prayers to the saints and if they had been aware of the ancient custom of prayers for the dead, they might have changed their minds. They did know, however, that Saint Augustine, one of their favorite theologians, spoke eloquently about prayers for the holy souls and about the value of Mass offered for them.

Our own foundress, Saint Catherine of Genoa, wrote the most beautiful and inspiring work on purgatory, which paradoxically was very popular with Protestant holiness writers of the nineteenth century (see *Catherine of Genoa*).

Quotation for Meditation
The following selection makes clear that Saint Augustine not only prayed for his mother and father but also asked others to pray for them so that after death they might be released from their sins.

[M]y brother said something to the effect that he would be happier if she were to die in her own land and not in a strange country. But as she heard this she looked at him anxiously, restraining him with her eye because he savored of earthly things, and then she looked at me and said: "See the way he talks." And then she said to us both: "Lay this body wherever it may be. Let no care of it disturb you: this only I ask of you that you should remember me at the altar of the Lord wherever you may be…."

Thus, my Glory and my Life, God of my heart, leaving aside for this time her good deeds, for which I give thanks to Thee in joy, I now pray to Thee for my mother's sins. Grant my prayer through the true Medicine of our wounds, who hung upon the cross and who now sitting at Thy right hand makes intercession for us. I know that she dealt mercifully, and from her heart forgave those who trespassed against her; do Thou also forgive such trespasses as she may have been guilty of in all the years since her baptism; forgive them, Lord, forgive them, I beseech Thee: enter not into judgment with her. Let Thy mercy be exalted above Thy justice, for Thy words are true and Thou hast promised that the merciful shall obtain mercy….

So let her rest in peace, together with her husband, for she had no other before nor after him, but served him, in patience bringing forth fruit for Thee, and winning him likewise for Thee. And inspire, O my Lord my God, inspire Thy servants my brethren. Thy sons my masters, whom I serve with heart and voice and pen, that as many of them as read this may remember at Thy altar Thy servant Monica, with Patricius, her husband, by whose bodies Thou didst bring me into this life, though how I know not. May they with loving mind remember these who were my parents in this transitory light, my brethren who serve Thee as our Father in our Catholic mother, and those who are to be fellow citizens with me in the eternal Jerusalem, which Thy people sigh for in their pilgrimage from birth until they come there; so that what my mother at her end asked of me may be fulfilled more richly in the prayers of so many gained for her by my Confessions than by my prayers alone.

— Saint Augustine, *Confessions*, IX, 11, 13;
See also *Catechism of the Catholic Church*, nn. 1030–1032

∾ Quiet Time and Then Discussion ∾

Questions for Meditation

1. Do I remember to pray for the dead?
2. Do I ask them to pray for me and the world we live in?
3. Do I invite others to remember and pray for those who have gone before us, whether they are already saints in heaven or holy souls on their way?

Prayer

O Lord Jesus Christ, You have redeemed all who are saved by Your holy death and Precious Blood. Help us to be purified of every stain and imperfection of will so that we may accept the fullness of Your redemption and fulfill in ourselves the just penance for our sins. Amen.

The Saints in Heaven

READINGS:
Ephesians 1:17–18; Hebrews 11:32–12:3;
Hebrews 12:22–24; Revelation 21:10–11, 22

At the present time, when faith is weakened by worldliness, it is not surprising that even believers reflect ideas about the eternal life of the saints that are spiritually inconsistent and theologically silly. Our brothers and sisters who are saints live a life of total charity with God and one another, toward us on earth and toward the holy souls, who are still on the way to heaven. It is a mystery how any being, even God in eternal life, can think of our limited and time-bound world, but we know from the Scriptures that God — Father, Son, and Holy Spirit — indeed watches over us. We also know that the saints, led by our Blessed Mother, pray for this sad world, where good and evil are locked in a duel for souls.

What we know about the saints is that their whole existence is filled with the Paschal Mystery, that is, the loving worship of Christ in His humanity as He offers to the Godhead the worship of all creation sanctified by His loving and obedient sacrifice on the Cross.

At this juncture of salvation history the saints in heaven (and the holy souls in purgatory) are without their bodies. The Church Fathers teach that at the end of the world we will all be reunited with our bodies. The glory of the saints will be greater and complete, and the pains of the lost will be more acute. Let us pray that the latter will be very few and that we will not be among them. In the meantime we see from Scripture that the saints and angels all seem very concerned about the battle for souls going on in this valley of tears. Every day we should ask the intercession of our heavenly friends, just as we ask good people on earth to pray for us. We should study the lives of the saints and holy people and try to imitate their love of God and service to others.

Quotation for Meditation

Why should our praise and glorification, or even the celebration of this feast day mean anything to the saints? What do they care about earthly honors when their heavenly Father honors them by fulfilling the faithful promise of the Son? What does our commendation mean to them? The saints have no need of honor from us; neither does our devotion add the slightest thing to what is theirs. Clearly, if we venerate their memory, it serves us, not them. But I tell you, when I think of them, I feel myself inflamed by a tremendous yearning.

Calling the saints to mind inspires, or rather arouses in us above all else, a longing to enjoy their company, so desirable in itself. We long to share in the citizenship of heaven, to dwell with the spirits of the blessed, to join the assembly of patriarchs, the ranks of the prophets, the council of apostles, the great host of martyrs, the noble company of confessors, and the choir of virgins. In short, we long to be united in happiness with all the saints....

Come, brothers, let us at length spur ourselves on. We must rise again with Christ, we must seek the world which is above and set our mind on the things of heaven. Let us long for those who are longing for us, hasten to those who are waiting for us, and ask those who look for our coming to intercede for us....

When we commemorate the saints, we are inflamed with another yearning: that Christ our life may also appear to us as he appeared to them and that we may one day share in his glory. Until then we see him, not as he is, but as he became for our sake.

He is our head, crowned not with glory, but with the thorns of our sins. As members of that head, crowned with thorns, we should be ashamed to live in luxury; his purple robes are a mockery rather than an honor. When Christ comes again, his death shall no longer be proclaimed, and we shall know that we also have died, and that our life is hidden with him. The glorious head of the Church will appear and his glorified members will shine in splendor with him, when he forms this lowly body anew into such glory as belongs to himself, its head.

— Saint Bernard of Clairvaux, Sermon for All Saints' Day,
Liturgy of the Hours, IV, 1526–1527

⟋ Quiet Time and Then Discussion ⟋

Questions for Meditation

1. Do I at least occasionally think of the saints and ask their intercession?
2. Do I have any favorite saints and do I know why they are saints?
3. Who is my favorite saint?

Prayer

Lord Jesus, You are given glory by Your saints, brothers and sisters to us, who are still poor suffering souls. Even in eternal glory they think of us. Hear the prayers of the canonized saints, but also those of multitudes of uncanonized saints. With Your loving help and forgiveness we will someday be with them. Amen.

The Queen of All Saints

READINGS:
Genesis 3:15; Luke 1:26–38; John 19:25–27; Revelation 12:1–6

We cannot leave our consideration of the communion of saints without prayerfully turning our attention to the unique place of the Mother of God in the plan of salvation and in the Church. It is regrettable that the Protestant Reformation eventually turned away from the ancient teaching of the early Church about Mary as the Mother of the God-Man and Mother of the Church. In the second century Saint Irenaeus called Mary the new Eve and Mother of the new race of the children of God, that is, Mother of the Church or the Mystical Body of Christ. The oldest Marian devotional book, the *Protoevangelium* of James, copied into all known Christian languages, dates from the end of the second century. The oldest known prayer to Mary, "We fly to thy protection, holy Mother of God …" comes from

Egypt in the following century. In Genesis 3:15, Mary is shown to be an essential part of salvation history, and her unique role is proclaimed in the Book of Revelation 12:1–6.

Luther and Calvin wrote devoutly of the Blessed Mother, and Zwingli even included the Hail Mary in the first prayer book of his new Reformed Church. As popular religious expressions sometimes do, certain Marian devotions moved toward superstition. This led Saint Louis de Montfort, the great Marian apostle, to teach that any devotion to Mary not based on her unique relationship to her divine Son was "idolatry." Despite occasional devotional excess, the Catholic and Orthodox Churches continue to acknowledge the dogmatic teaching of the Council of Ephesus: Mary is the mother of the Person who is the divine Son of God.

Mary stands at the center of the communion of saints. She was given to us by her Son as our Mother as she stood at the foot of the Cross. No Catholic need ever apologize for devotion to Mary. She herself prophesied that all generations would call her blessed.

Quotations for Meditation

Mary's role in the Church is inseparable from her union with Christ and flows directly from it. "This union of the mother with the Son in the work of salvation is made manifest from the time of Christ's virginal conception up to his death";[18] it is made manifest above all at the hour of his passion:

> Thus the Blessed Virgin advanced in her pilgrimage of faith, and faithfully persevered in her union with her Son unto the cross. There she stood, in keeping with the divine plan, enduring with her only-begotten Son the intensity of his suffering, joining herself with his sacrifice in her mother's heart, and lovingly consenting to the immolation of this victim, born of her: to be given, by the same Christ Jesus dying on the cross, as a mother to his disciple, with these words: "Woman, behold your son."[19]
>
> — *Catechism of the Catholic Church*, n. 964

By her complete adherence to the Father's will, to his Son's redemptive work, and to every prompting of the Holy Spirit, the Virgin Mary is the Church's model of faith and charity. Thus she is a "preeminent and ... wholly unique member of the Church"; indeed, she is the "exemplary realization" (*typus*)[20] of the Church.

— *Catechism of the Catholic Church*, n. 967

Her role in relation to the Church and to all humanity goes still further. "In a wholly singular way she cooperated by her obedience, faith, hope, and burning charity in the Savior's work of restoring supernatural life to souls. For this reason she is a mother to us in the order of grace."[21]

— *Catechism of the Catholic Church*, n. 968

"This motherhood of Mary in the order of grace continues uninterruptedly from the consent which she loyally gave at the Annunciation and which she sustained without wavering beneath the cross, until the eternal fulfillment of all the elect. Taken up to heaven, she did not lay aside this saving office but by her manifold intercession continues to bring us the gifts of eternal salvation…. Therefore the Blessed Virgin is invoked in the Church under the titles of Advocate, Helper, Benefactress, and Mediatrix."[22]

— *Catechism of the Catholic Church*, n. 969

"Mary's function as mother of men in no way obscures or diminishes this unique mediation of Christ, but rather shows its power. But the Blessed Virgin's salutary influence on men … flows forth from the superabundance of the merits of Christ, rests on his mediation, depends entirely on it, and draws all its power from it."[23] "No creature could ever be counted along with the Incarnate Word and Redeemer; but just as the priesthood of Christ is shared in various ways both by his ministers and the faithful, and as the one goodness of God is radiated in different ways among his creatures, so also the unique mediation of the Redeemer does not exclude but rather gives rise to a manifold cooperation which is but a sharing in this one source."[24]

— *Catechism of the Catholic Church*, n. 970

⚘ Quiet Time and Then Discussion ⚘

Questions for Meditation

1. Do you think of Mary as your spiritual mother?
2. Do you ask her intercession for yourself and all those you care about?
3. How would you explain Catholic and Orthodox devotion to Mary beginning with the earliest centuries of the Church?

Prayer

Mary, mother of the Church and my mother, I ask you humbly and confidently to intercede for me, my family and friends, the Church, and the whole world. How beautiful it is that the Son of God would be your Son with all that that word means. At the wedding feast of Cana you seem to have changed His mind. Mary, I have many needs, many troubles. I am concerned for the welfare of so many. Please pray for me, pray for us all. Amen.

The Forgiveness of Sins

READINGS:
Psalm 16; Matthew 16:17–20; Mark 2:1–12;
Luke 22:31–34; Colossians 3:5–17

That God forgives sins is clearly seen in the Jewish Scriptures (the Old Testament) as well as in the Gospels and other New Testament writings. We do not earn forgiveness or demand it of God, because He has already promised it to us. He gives us the grace to ask to be forgiven (prevenient grace), and He summons us to repentance in so many ways. It is interesting that the idea of divine forgiveness is not found in the traditional old religions we may still encounter in remote parts of Africa and Asia. Tribal people may actually be quite religious and define all aspects of life by religious belief, but they do not believe their sins can be forgiven, because all they know of God comes from nature. They can know God's almighty power and His divinity (Romans

1:20), but God's mercy and forgiveness are known only by His revelation.

Our knowledge of God's willingness to forgive comes to us from Christ, who joins the forgiveness of sin with Baptism in the name of the Father, Son, and Holy Spirit, one God (see Matthew 28:19). Baptism is the unique road to complete forgiveness, so that a newly baptized adult, though required to repent of his previous sins, is not obliged to confess them. Sins committed after Baptism can be forgiven if the person is truly repentant. To realize this, we have only to look at Christ's example of forgiving Saint Peter and the other apostles, and remember the constant call of Saint Paul and other New Testament writers to their baptized converts to repent. In subsequent meditations we will consider the beautiful Sacrament of Reconciliation. It is important to recall that Christ explicitly gave the apostles the power in His name to communicate His divine forgiveness (John 20:22–23). At the same time He gave them the ability to withhold forgiveness from those who are not truly repentant.

How beautiful and consoling is the gift of forgiveness. Looking back on their earlier days, Christians sometimes feel they are not forgiven. Any complete act of repentance, even if we cannot recall all specific past sins, returns the most sinful soul to the state of grace when they receive the Sacrament of Reconciliation. If it is not possible to receive the sacrament, the Church teaches that repentance arising from real regret for having offended the loving God makes the person open to receive the grace of divine forgiveness and to return to God's friendship. None of this is easy or cheap love, nor is it just God being nice. It is founded entirely on Christ's sacrifice on the Cross. He has satisfied justice by taking on our sins.

Quotation for Meditation

O Lord, "I am Thy servant; I am Thy servant and the son of Thy handmaid. Thou hast broken my bonds. I will sacrifice to Thee the sacrifice of praise." Let my heart and my tongue praise Thee, and "let all my bones say, O Lord, who is like to Thee?" Let them say and do Thou answer me and say to my soul: "I am Thy salvation." Who am I and what kind of man am I? What evil has there not been in my deeds, or if not in my deeds, in my words, or if not in my words, then in my will? But You, Lord, are good and merciful, and Your right hand had regard to the profundity of my death and drew out the abyss of corruption that was in the bottom of my heart. By Your gift I had come totally not to will what I willed but to will what You willed. But where in all that long time was my free will, and from what deep sunken hiding-place was it suddenly summoned forth in the moment in which

I bowed my neck to Your easy yoke and my shoulders to Your light burden, Christ Jesus, my Helper and my Redeemer? How lovely I suddenly found it to be free from the loveliness of those vanities, so that now it was a joy to renounce what I had been so afraid to lose. For You cast them out of me, O true and supreme Loveliness, You cast them out of me and took their place in me, You who are sweeter than all pleasure, yet not to flesh and blood; brighter than all light, yet deeper within than any secret; loftier than all honor, but not to those who are lofty to themselves. Now my mind was free from the cares that had gnawed it, from aspiring and getting and weltering in filth and rubbing the scab of lust. And I talked with You as friends talk, my glory and my riches and my salvation, my Lord God.

— Saint Augustine, *Confessions*, IX, 1

Quiet Time and Then Discussion

Questions for Meditation

1. Do I sometimes think with loving gratitude of God's forgiveness of my sins?
2. Do I realize that in some mysterious way Christ has paid the price for my sins?

3. When I meet others who are burdened with guilt and self-hatred, do I seriously suggest that they spend time in prayer and receive the Sacrament of Reconciliation?

Prayer

Lord Jesus, You paid the price for the world's salvation and for mine as well. I am mostly ungrateful for Your gift, Your endless and ongoing gift of forgiveness. As I struggle daily with my sins and failings, I am more aware of Your love for me and for all poor sinners. This realization should make me all the more forgiving and understanding of my fellow sinners on the way to eternal life. May You have mercy on us all. Amen.

The Resurrection of the Body

READINGS:
John 5:25–29; Romans 8:5–11; 1 Corinthians 15:35–37.
See also Catechism of the Catholic Church, *nn. 988–1019.*

When someone dies, it is very noticeable that those who hardly ever practice their faith, or any faith at all, will speak of the hope of life after death, often in very Christian terms. They believe that their dear one lives on and is with God in a place of joy and peace. While all this may appear to be simply wish fulfillment or sentimentality, since it is the only shred of belief they seem to have, their hopes suggest a very real place at which to begin evangelization. Our Savior tells us to get ready because death will come unexpectedly and, with it, the Last Judgment, when we will render an account of our lives to Him.

Based on clear Scriptural arguments (only a few of many texts are given above), the Catholic faith teaches that not only do we survive death without our bodies (a mystery) but that at the end of the ages we will also be reunited with our bodies in some real way. Nevertheless, Saint Paul tells us that we will be changed, and he uses the mysterious expression that we will have a spiritual body. Speculation about what this means ranges from silly cartoons of the saints standing with halos and wings on fluffy clouds to questions related to the risen body of Our Lord. His body passed through locked doors and appears to have moved from place to place without the need for what we think of as travel.

While those of little faith hope to survive death, they may have a great deal of trouble with the idea that at the end of the ages the whole human race will rise in what are their own changed, or spiritual, bodies. Since this truth, which Our Lord taught and Saint Paul emphasized, is filled with mystery, it is best to leave it in the realm of the mysterious and move to simple belief, that is, to acceptance of the mystery on the authority of God's word.

Quotations for Meditation

A great thing was being done when God constructed humans from matter. It was honored as often as it experienced the hand of God, when He touched it, when He pulled at it, when He formed and shaped it. Reflect on God, totally occupied and given over to it, with His hand, His senses, His work, His counsel and wisdom, His providence, and especially His affection that guided its features. For, whatever was expressed in clay, it was Christ, the future man, that was thought of, for He, the Word made flesh, was then clay and earth.

— Tertullian, *De Resurrectione Mortuorum*, VI, 2–4, quoted in
Land of the Living: A Theology of the Last Things, 155

The dust around us will one day become animate. We may ourselves be dead long before, and not see it. We ourselves may elsewhere be buried, and, should it be our exceeding blessedness to rise to life eternal, we may rise in other places, far in the east or west. But, as God's word is sure, what is sown is raised; the earth to earth, ashes to ashes, dust to dust, shall become glory to glory, and life to the living God, and a true incorruptible image of the spirit made perfect. Here the saints sleep, here they shall rise. A great sight will a Christian country then be, if earth remains what it is; when holy places pour out the worshippers who have for generations kept vigil therein, waiting through the long night for the bright coming of Christ!

— John Henry Newman,
Parochial and Plains Sermons, I, 21

 Quiet Time and Then Discussion

Questions for Meditation

1. Does Christ's frequent admonition to prepare for death really affect my life?

2. Do I console others, as Saint Paul suggests, with the promise of eternal life in Christ at times of serious sickness and death?

3. Do I make use of the grief of others to teach them about our hope in the resurrection of the body?

Prayer

Lord Jesus Christ, You have promised those who believe and follow You that they will come with You to our Father's house. We forget this promise in the events, even the deeply meaningful events, of daily life. Every time we receive You in the Holy Eucharist, we proclaim not only Your death and resurrection but also our hope of life with You in our Father's house and our complete survival after death. Increase our faith and help us to be Your instruments to encourage faith in others. Help us all to know that we will be like You because we shall see You as You are forever and ever. Amen.

Meditation Thirty-One

I Believe in Life Everlasting (#1):
The Particular and General Judgments

READINGS:

*Luke 16:19–31; Matthew 16:24–28; Hebrews 9:27–28;
Matthew 25 (all). See also* Catechism of the
Catholic Church, *nn. 1020–1022.*

Is there any Christian teaching more neglected than Christ's own reaffirmation of the Old Testament teaching that we are judged by God at the end of our lives and that in the next world we live out the results of that judgment in a very real way? The study of what happens after death is called eschatology, or the study of the last things: judgment, heaven, purgatory, and hell. This study, so often neglected and sometimes denied by being ignored, is a most important part of our faith because it directly pertains to our eternal destiny and that of those we love.

The New Testament readings, some of which we have indicated here, make clear that our eternal destiny — either life with God or the "darkness where there will be the weeping and gnashing of teeth" — will be determined at death. Since no one has the ability to think directly or adequately of the eternal or everlasting, it is in some sense impossible for us to assess the full meaning of life after death, of heaven and hell. Don't feel bad about that, because it is even more impossible for the unbeliever to think of oblivion. Both the Bible and common sense tell us that our eternal destiny must begin when we leave this world. This destiny initially affects only our soul, that is, our spiritual personhood, because our bodies return to dust until the end of the ages, as we saw in the previous meditation. Our Lord makes clear in His parables and direct teaching that the soul is judged and assigned its destiny immediately after we leave this world. He says to the good thief, "Today you will be with me in paradise" (Luke 23:43). He also indicates that there are sins that can be forgiven in the world to come (Matthew 12:32). Yet we know that no one can enter the heavenly Jerusalem with any imperfection (Revelation 22:3–5). Hence we believe that purification necessary for entrance into heaven can occur in the next world.

We also know from both Old and New Testaments that there is eternal punishment. From the earliest times Christians have believed that the saved and the lost are assigned their different destinies at death. Our Lord teaches that He did not come to judge the world but to save the world and that the lost condemn themselves. We must realize that our judgment is not an arbitrary decision of God; rather it flows necessarily from the mystery of good and evil and from the freedom of the human will. Finally we must recall that from those to whom much is given, much is expected. This all helps to put this life in a realistic perspective.

Quotations for Meditation

[The Lord] ascended into heaven, whence He shall come again with glory to judge the living and the dead, each receiving according to his own merits. Those who have responded to the Love and Mercy of God will go to eternal life; those who have rejected that Love and Mercy to the end will go to the fire that will have no end.

— Pope Paul VI, *Credo of the People of God* (1968)

Since, however, we know not the day nor the hour, on Our Lord's advice we must be constantly vigilant, so that having finished the course of our earthly life, we may merit to enter into the marriage feast with Him and be numbered among the blessed (cf. Matthew 25:31–46) and that we may not be ordered to go into eternal fire like the wicked and slothful servant (cf. Matthew 25:41), in the exterior darkness where "there will be the weeping and the gnashing of teeth" (Matthew 22:13 and 25:30). For before we reign with Christ in glory, all of us will be made manifest "before the tribunal of Christ, so that each one may receive what he has won through the body, according to his works, whether good or evil" (2 Corinthians 5:10) and at the end of the world "they who have done good shall come forth unto resurrection of life; but those who have done evil unto resurrection of judgment" (John 5:29; cf. Matthew 25:46).

— *Lumen Gentium*, 48

Quiet Time and Then Discussion

Questions for Meditation

1. Do I think of the inescapable fact that I shall be judged according to my deeds?
2. Is my life directed by the certainty of God's judgment?
3. Do I ever remind others that they too shall be judged?

Prayer

Lord Jesus, give me the grace of the Holy Spirit, that I may always live my days preparing for the Last Judgment, as You have taught us to do. In my thoughts and prayers help me to move beyond the swirl of sensations, desires, sorrows, and joys of this life and consider the great and awesome destiny to which You call me. Help me recall that this life is a journey and not a destination. And through Your Holy Spirit encourage others to consider the things to come in Your heavenly kingdom. Amen.

Meditation Thirty-Two

I Believe in Life Everlasting (#2): Purgatory Is the Purification of the Soul

READINGS:
2 Maccabees 12:46; Matthew 12:31–32.
See also Catechism of the Catholic Church, *nn. 1030–1032;*
John Henry Newman, The Dream of Gerontius.

The Jews and early Christians prayed that the souls of the dead would come into the fullness of eternal life. In other words, they hoped that their sins would be forgiven in the world to come, as Our Lord had indicated when speaking about the sin against the Holy Spirit. Both Catholic and Orthodox Christians have always prayed for the dead on their journey of purification. The name purgatory, which means purification, came to be applied in medieval times to this stage of our journey toward God, although the earliest Christian writers and Church Fathers wrote of this reality and the need to pray for the dead. The term itself comes from Saint Augustine, who speaks of the purging pains of this state of being.

The Church's teaching on the cleansing of purgatory has the full authority of the Council of Florence (1439) and the Council of Trent (1563). We also have the witness of the saints, who considered it a great act of charity to pray for the dead, that we might bring them "some consolation," as Saint John Chrysostom said. Unfortunately, artists and poets like Dante have dramatized the purifying sufferings of purgatory and made it sound like another hell, rather than a passage to heaven. The Council of Trent issued a condemnation of such horror stories. The Holy Souls (the proper description of these travelers to heaven) are in a state of perfect love of God. They joyfully accept His will and have achieved a level of peace beyond the greatest saints who would still be in this world.

Much of the Church's popular teaching on purgatory comes from the revelation of our foundress of the Oratory, Saint Catherine of Genoa. Oratorians should be familiar with her teaching and should encourage others to pray for the dead. They should also prepare for their own journey by purifying their spiritual lives, cooperating as best they can with Christ's saving grace, and doing penance to reduce the punishment for sin. Christ has paid the total price for our salvation, but in the parables and especially in the teaching about bad feelings toward others, He indicates that we must do our own part (Luke 12:57–58).

Quotation for Meditation

As she dwelt on this love, the condition of the souls of the faithful in purgatory, where they are cleansed of the remaining rust and stain of sin, became clear to her. She rejoiced in her union with God in this loving purgatory, and so did the souls in purgatory, she realized, who have no choice but to be there, and this because of God's just decree.

These souls cannot think,
"I am here, and justly so because of my sins,"
or "I wish I had never committed such sins
for now I would be in paradise,"
or "That person there is leaving before me,"
or "I will leave before that other one."
They cannot remember the good and evil
in their past nor that of others.
Such is their joy in God's will, in His pleasure,
that they have no concern for themselves
but dwell only on their joy in God's ordinance,

in having Him do what He will.
They see only the goodness of God,
His mercy toward men.
Should they be aware of other good or evil,
theirs would not be perfect charity.
They do not see that their suffering
is due to their sins,
for that awareness would be a want of perfection,
and in purgatory souls cannot sin.
Only once do the souls understand
the reason for their purgatory:
the moment in which they leave this life.
After that moment, that knowledge disappears.
Immersed in charity, incapable of deviating from it,
they can only will or desire pure love.
There is no joy save that in paradise
to be compared to the joy of the souls in purgatory.
This joy increases day by day
because of the way in which the love of God
corresponds to that of the soul,
since the impediment to that love is worn away daily.
This impediment is the rust of sin....

As for paradise, God has placed no doors there.
Whoever wishes to enter, does so.
All-merciful God stands there with His arms open,
waiting to receive us into His glory.
I also see, however,
that the divine essence is so pure and light-filled —
much more than we can imagine —
that the soul that has but the slightest imperfection
would rather throw itself into a thousand hells
than appear thus before the divine presence.
Tongue cannot express nor heart understand
the full meaning of purgatory,
which the soul willingly accepts as a mercy,
the realization that that suffering is of no importance
compared to the removal of the impediment of sin.
The greatest suffering of the souls in purgatory,
it seems to me, is their awareness
that something in them displeases God,
that they have deliberately
gone against His great goodness....

All that I have said
is as nothing compared to what I feel within,
the witnessed correspondence of love

between God and the Soul;
for when God sees the Soul pure as it was in its origins,
He tugs at it with a glance,
draws it and binds it to Himself with a fiery love
that by itself could annihilate the immortal soul.
In so acting, God so transforms the soul in Him
that it knows nothing other than God;
and He continues to draw it up into His fiery love
until He restores it
to that pure state from which it first issued.
As it is being drawn upwards,
the soul feels itself melting
in the fire of that love of its sweet God,
for He will not cease
until He has brought the soul to its perfection.
That is why the soul seeks to cast off
any and all impediments,
so that it can be lifted up to God;
and such impediments
are the cause of the suffering of the souls in purgatory....

And I see rays of lightning
darting from that divine love to the creature,
so intense and fiery as to annihilate not the body alone

but, were it possible, the soul.
These rays purify and then annihilate.
The soul becomes like gold
that becomes purer as it is fired,
all dross being cast out.

— *Catherine of Genoa*, 71–72, 78–79

≈ Quiet Time and Then Discussion ≈

Questions for Meditation

1. Do I seriously pray for the Holy Souls, especially those whom I love?
2. Do I make an effort to have Masses offered for them and for those who have no one to pray for them?
3. Do I think of my own journey after death?

Prayer

Perfect Peace (from the Coptic Liturgy)

To these, O Lord, and to all those of whom we make remembrance, and to those also of whom each one thinks in his own heart, give rest in the bosom of Abraham, Isaac, and Jacob. Give them refreshment in the smiling fields of the Paradise of peace where there is neither sorrow nor pain. Grant to them the good things Thou hast promised, which eye has not seen nor ear heard. They have indeed sinned through ignorance and forgetfulness, for they were but men, living in this world and weighed down by the burden of a fleshly nature. O Thou who art a God of goodness and the friend of man, deign to pardon them, for there is no man on earth, even if his life were but of one day, who is not stained with sin.

— *PRAYING IN THE PRESENCE OF OUR LORD*
FOR THE HOLY SOULS, 29

Meditation Thirty-Three

I Believe in Life Everlasting (#3):
Hell or the Eternal Loss of God

READINGS:
Matthew 25:41–46; Luke 16:19–31;
Mark 9:42–50; Revelation 21:5–8.
See also Catechism of the Catholic Church, *nn. 1033–1037.*

Allof God's mysteries are mysteries of light, but two of the
mysteries of faith are mysteries of impenetrable darkness: sin
and eternal punishment. Our concept of God, derived from
Scripture and even from reason, seems to tell us that the God of
goodness and love could not send a human soul forever into a
dark pit of terrible punishment and complete frustration of all
desire — a kind of black hole. On the other hand, Scripture
makes it very clear that there is eternal punishment, what Our
Lord refers to as the "everlasting flames prepared for the devil and

his angels." Many of Christ's parables refer to everlasting punishment, as do a number of New Testament writers, including, in very dramatic terms, the author of the Book of Revelation. Perhaps when we think of the atrocities of the twentieth century — Auschwitz, the gulag in Russia, and the diabolical activities of some human beings — it is easier to cope with the idea of eternal punishment.

Some ages have thought it was common for people to be lost forever, while others, like our own, have tended to treat eternal punishment like a remote possibility. But Christ's warnings in the Gospel remain, and they must always be taken seriously because, as the Church teaches about the Scriptures, these words are given by God to lead us on our journey to eternal life.

Saint Faustina Kowalska, the mystic nun of Divine Mercy, wrote that Our Savior revealed to her that He calls to every soul at the moment of death. This is a pure unmerited grace. According to Saint Faustina, the soul is still capable of either turning to God's call or rejecting it and perishing in hell. This is a last and real call of grace. A number of theologians have also raised this possibility and have used the example of the good thief. Whatever the reality is, we must take Our Lord's warnings about hell very seriously.

Quotation for Meditation

[T]he state of punishment visited on the sinner is not merely the negation, but the reverse, of divine glorification, and in its way is as supernatural and mysterious as the latter. It, too, is a sort of supernatural transfiguration of nature, accomplished by the fiery power of the divinity, not in the positive sense that the sinner's nature is transformed into a sun shining with the light of glory and radiant with happiness, but in a negative sense, so far as nature, without being actually annihilated, is so utterly degraded, so completely stifled and laid waste, that it incessantly perceives and feels itself hovering on the brink of annihilation. The appalling frightfulness of this state consists in the fact that the creature not only tortures itself by the inner conflict of its malice and its unsatisfied appetites, but is plunged into a vastly deeper sea of misery and unhappiness by a supernatural force which lays hold of it and imprisons it, so that it succumbs to the weight of a supernatural, overpowering action from without. It is devastated by an external agent even more that it devastates itself.

— Matthias Joseph Scheeben,
The Mysteries of Christianity, 686–687

Quiet Time and Then Discussion

Questions for Meditation

1. Do I think often enough of Our Lord's warning about eternal punishment?
2. Do I warn, as best I can, those who have put His warnings aside?
3. Do I pray for the salvation of those who are apparently far away from God and salvation?

Prayer

Lord Jesus Christ, Our Savior, You died to save us from eternal ruin. You taught us the way to eternal life and preached this way in Your Gospel. Send Your Holy Spirit with His divine power, especially to those who have lost their way. Deliver us from eternal death by Your grace and call to all who are in terrible danger. Amen.

Meditation Thirty-Four

I Believe in Life Everlasting (#4)

READINGS:
Matthew 25:31–40; Mark 13:21–27;
Luke 9:26–27; John 14:1–4;
Revelation 21:1–8

Most human beings hope that there is a better life beyond the present one — a life of blessings for those have done good. A recent poll indicates that 92 percent of all Americans believe this. No sane person can hope that this is not so. No one can wish for oblivion, but sadly, some see no other possibility after death. The universal hope for a better afterlife is not the same as the Christian hope; the latter is based on divine revelation in the Scriptures, especially in the New Testament. Our Lord's words tell us of an afterlife that is eternal. It is revealed as a place of peace, our Father's house, paradise, a kingdom and place prepared for the saved since the beginning of the world.

For Christians the word "heaven" signifies the fulfillment of the deepest desires of the human heart, the hope for supreme happiness, which is more accurately termed blessedness. Christ's promise indicates that eternal life is something personal and individual. It is not to be thought of as some oriental religions envision it, that is, as a state in which the individual must be absorbed like a drop of water in an infinite sea of being. One of Christianity's essential teachings is that personhood or individuality are not obstacles to holiness or our eternal destiny, although egotism certainly is. The words of Christ, who alone has come down from the Father, indicate that our survival of death is very personal. "And when I go and prepare a place for you, I will come again and will take you to myself, that where I am you may be also" (John 14:3–4).

We are clearly told by Saint Paul (1 Corinthians 2:9) that in this world we cannot conceive of what God has prepared in the next for those who love Him. Many artists, especially in the Middle Ages, have tried to depict the unthinkable as a way of teaching and inspiring believers. All these works, however, fall short of giving an essential image of eternal life. Saint Augustine reminds us: eye has not seen it, because it has no color; ear has not heard it, because it makes no sound; and our hearts have to enter the mystery, not the reverse.

Since eternal life is beyond human comprehension, it is a subject of faith, something to be believed in, like the other mysteries of faith. Once we accept the revelation of God in Christ, we can move with the greatest consolation toward eternal life with the images Jesus has given us. Choose one you find most meaningful. For me, eternity is the promise to live in my Father's house.

Quotation for Meditation

O lovely and luminous house, "I have loved your beauty and the place where the glory dwells of my Lord," who made it and possesses it. In my pilgrimage may I sigh for you; and I ask of Him who made you that He should possess me too in you…. "I have gone astray like a sheep that is lost," but I hope that I may be brought back to You on the shoulders of my Shepherd, your Builder….

Jerusalem, my Fatherland, Jerusalem which is my mother: and remembering Thee its Ruler, its Light, its Father and Tutor and Spouse, its pure and strong Delight, its Joy unshakable and the sum of all ineffable good because Thou alone art the one supreme and true Good. I shall not turn away but shall come to the peace of that Jerusalem, my dear mother, where are the first-fruits of my spirit, from which all certitude comes to me….

There Thou shalt collect from my present scatteredness and deformity all that I am, and Thou shalt re-form me and confirm me unto eternity, O my God, my Mercy.

— Saint Augustine, *Confessions*, XII, 15, 16

Quiet Time and Then Discussion

Questions for Meditation

1. In the difficulties of life do I pause to remember that "the sufferings of this life are not to be compared with the glory that is to come"?

2. In hours of sorrow and mourning, am I willing and able to encourage others with a truly Christian idea of heaven?

3. Do I use my faith to confront the fear everyone has of death and of what is on the other side?

Prayer

O Lord Jesus Christ, You are Lord of life and death. You alone can speak the words of eternal life. Fill me with the wisdom of Your Holy Spirit and grant that I may believe and know that we have here no lasting city but that we seek one that is to come. In my own small way may I, like the apostles, bear witness to the life that is to come. Amen.

Meditation Thirty-Five

I Believe in Life Everlasting (#5):
The New Heaven and the New Earth

READINGS:
2 Peter 3:11–13; 2 Thessalonians 1:10–12;
Revelation 20:11–15; 21:1–8

One of the most fascinating and inspiring doctrines of the Christian faith is one we hardly ever hear of or think about. When we think about the afterlife, we think about its wonderful and dreadful possibilities, but these are not the ultimate condition of human beings. For human beings who are saved in Christ, eternal life begins at the hour of death, either with entrance into eternal glory, or with a time of final purification, which is really a passage to heaven itself. But there is still the resurrection of the body, and the reuniting of the body and soul to achieve the final triumph over death, or the complete victory of

Christ's grace within us. This is the final victory, when we shall be mysteriously transformed into the image of Christ.

The victory that began at Baptism and, with twists and turns, and ups and downs, went on during our earthly life, was perfected at once by our entrance into eternal life. The victory will come to completion in a "new heaven and a new earth." When we think of the coming of a new heaven and a new earth, of course our attention is drawn to the apocalyptic scenes of the Last Judgment and the dissolving of the present universe in fire. We are intrigued by the thought of the Last Judgment, when the final justice of God will be vindicated before all who have ever lived, the saved or the lost. Our Lord, Saint Peter, Saint Paul, as well as the author of the Book of Revelation tell us of this great judgment at the end of the world. The *Catechism of the Catholic Church* gives these texts and others too numerous to list here (nn. 1038–1050). Our imaginations tend to dwell on this because the scene of the great judgment is so fascinating, but like all things in eternity, it is incomprehensible. But to stop here may lead to a kind of morbid preoccupation with the end of the cosmos and the judgment of the wicked.

Our Christian vocation calls us to grow in the image of Christ, and then we shall join our Savior as the Head of the Mystical Body in a totally transformed world. This is described by Saint Paul in imagery of extraordinary beauty and mystery.

> For the creation waits with eager longing for the revealing of the sons of God … the creation itself will be set free from its bondage to decay and obtain the glorious liberty of the children of God. We know that the whole creation has been groaning in travail together until now; and not only the creation, but we ourselves, who have the first fruits of the Spirit, groan inwardly as we wait for adoption as sons, the redemption of our bodies. (Romans 8:19–23)

So many human ills and sufferings are part of our physical reality, our bodies — sickness of all kinds, the effects of age, and many others. It is with the body, which includes the brain, that we grow in the image of Christ. This growth is ultimately rooted in the soul, which is the spiritual element joined to our body to make us human. The immortal soul rejoices in union with Christ at death, but at the end of the world, the body, with all creation, will be transformed. That is what is meant by the heavenly Jerusalem. In the course of our life of struggle and suffering, especially the suffering we endure for those whom we love, we should keep before our eyes the mysterious and lyrically beautiful symbols of the last chapters of Revelation — the new heaven and the new earth. Although quite beyond our comprehension, we have these hauntingly beautiful images. "[T]hey shall see his face, and his name shall be on their foreheads. And night shall be no more; they need no light of lamp or sun, for the Lord God will be their light, and they shall reign for ever and ever" (Revelation 22:4–5).

Quotation for Meditation

O Lord God, grant us peace, for Thou hast granted us all things, the peace of repose, the peace of Thy Sabbath, the peace that has no evening. For this gloriously beautiful order of things that are very good will pass away when it has achieved its end: it will have its morning and its evening.

But the seventh day is without evening. It has no sunset, for You sanctified it that it may abide forever. After all Your works which were very good, You rested on the seventh day — although You made them with no interruption of Your repose. And likewise the voice of Your book tells us that we also, after our works — which are only very good because You have granted us to accomplish them — will rest in You in the Sabbath of life everlasting.

— Saint Augustine, *Confessions*, XIII, 35, 36

∞ Quiet Time and Then Discussion ∞

Questions for Meditation

1. Do I ever spend time thinking about the world to come and the resurrection of the body?

2. Do I spend some time meditating on the reality, which is after all my final hope?

3. Does this mystery make me look at life and its struggles in a different way?

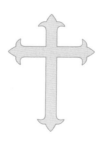

Prayer

O Eternal Son of God, You come from Eternity, from everlasting bliss, with Your Father and the Holy Spirit into this dark world. You suffered the worst that the world could do to You, but You will come at the end of the ages. Then our little world containing our whole person, body united with soul, will move from the passing of time unto the endless day of eternity. In the sufferings of life, help us to keep before our minds the glory that is to come, not only for ourselves, but for all who might suffer and those who turn to You in faith and the hope of salvation. Amen.

Notes

1. John C. Olin, *The Catholic Reformation: Savonarola to Ignatius Loyola* (New York: Harper & Row, 1969), 16.

2. See *Catherine of Genoa: Purgation and Purgatory, The Spiritual Dialogue*, trans. Serge Hughes; Introduction by Fr. Benedict J. Groeschel (Paulist Press, 1979).

3. Council of Chalcedon (451): DS 301; cf. Heb. 4:15.

4. Council of Chalcedon: DS 302.

5. Saint Augustine, *De civ. Dei*, 22, 17: PL 41, 779; cf. Saint Thomas Aquinas, *STh* III, 64, 2 *ad* 3.

6. LG 11; cf. Pius XII, *Mystici Corporis* (1943).

7. LG 11, § 2.

8. Cf. LG 10, § 2.

9. Cf. Jn. 20:21–23; Lk. 24:47; Mt. 28:18–20.

10. LG 8.

11. Cf. DS 2888.

12. Vatican Council I, *Dei Filius* 3: DS 3013.

13. See *Catherine of Genoa*.

14. See Ephesians 4:16.

15. See 1 Timothy 2:5.

16. Saint Dominic, dying, to his brothers.

[17] Saint Thérèse of Lisieux, *The Final Conversations*, trans. John Clarke (Washington, D.C.: ICS), 102.

[18] LG 57.

[19] LG 58; cf. Jn. 19:26–27.

[20] LG 53; 63.

[21] LG 61.

[22] LG 62.

[23] LG 60.

[24] LG 62.

Works Cited

In addition to Sacred Scripture and excerpts from the *Catechism of the Catholic Church*, the following published works are cited in this book.

Saint Augustine:
> *An Augustine Synthesis*, arr. Fr. Erich Przywara (Sheed and Ward, 1936)
> *Confessions*, trans. Frank Sheed (Sheed and Ward, 1944)
> *Works of Saint Augustine* (Vol. 5)
> *The Trinity*, trans. Edmund Hill, O.P. (New City Press, 1991)

Lincoln Barnett, *The Universe and Dr. Einstein*, with introduction by Albert Einstein (William Morrow and Company, 1948)

Bernard of Clairvaux, Sermon for All Saints' Day in *The Liturgy of the Hours*, IV (Catholic Book Publishing Company, 1975)

Catherine of Genoa: Purgation and Purgatory, The Spiritual Dialogue, trans. Serge Hughes; Introduction by Fr. Benedict J. Groeschel, C.F.R. (Paulist Press, 1979)

Jean-Pierre de Caussade, S.J., *Abandonment to Divine Providence*, trans. John Beevers (Doubleday/Image, 1975)

Benedict J. Groeschel, *Augustine: Major Writings* (Crossroad, 1995)

Romano Guardini, *The Lord*, trans. Elinor Castendyk Briefs (Regnery, 1982)

Pope John Paul II, *Wonders and Signs: The Miracles of Jesus* (Saint Paul Books & Media, 1990)

Francis Xavier Nguyễn Văn Thuận, *Testimony of Hope* (Pauline Books and Media, 2000)

Rev. James T. O'Connor: *Land of the Living: A Theology of the Last Things* (Catholic Book Publishing Co., 1992)

John Olin, *The Catholic Reformation: Savonarola to Ignatius Loyola* (Harper & Row, 1969)

Praying in the Presence of Our Lord for the Holy Souls, ed. Susan Tassone (OSV, 2001)

Matthias Joseph Scheeben, *The Mysteries of Christianity*, trans. Cyril Vollert, S.J. (B. Herder Book Co., 1946)

Tertullian, *De Resurrectione Mortuorum*, VI (cited in *Land of the Living: A Theology of the Last Things*)

George Weigel, *Witness to Hope* (Harper Collins, 1999)

Papal documents are taken from the Vatican website: www.vatican.va

Abbreviations:

The four major documents that issued from the Second Vatican Council are abbreviated as follows:

GS = *Gaudium et Spes*
LG = *Lumen Gentium*
PC = *Perfectae Caritatis*
SC = *Sacrosanctum Concilium*

For keys to other abbreviations, see indexes of the *Catechism of the Catholic Church.*

Contact Information

Oratory of Divine Love

For further information about the Oratory of Divine Love, go to their website, www.oratorydl.com, or write to:

Oratory of Divine Love
P.O. Box 1465
Bloomfield, NJ 07003

Franciscan Friars and Sisters of the Renewal

Contributions for the work of the Franciscan Friars and Sisters of the Renewal may be sent to:

Padre Pio Shelter
Fr. Benedict J. Groeschel, C.F.R.
Box 55
Larchmont, NY 10538